# CANTEENS AND HORSESHOES

## Relics of the Grand Army of the Republic

## DOUGLAS W. ROUSSIN

The opinions expressed in this manuscript are solely the opinions of the author and do not represent the opinions or thoughts of the publisher. The author has represented and warranted full ownership and/or legal right to publish all the materials in this book.

Canteens and Horseshoes
Relics of the Grand Army of the Republic
All Rights Reserved.
Copyright © 2014 Douglas W. Roussin
v3.0

Cover Photo © 2014 Douglas W. Roussin. All rights reserved - used with permission.

This book may not be reproduced, transmitted, or stored in whole or in part by any means, including graphic, electronic, or mechanical without the express written consent of the publisher except in the case of brief quotations embodied in critical articles and reviews.

Outskirts Press, Inc.
http://www.outskirtspress.com

ISBN: 978-1-4787-3011-8

Outskirts Press and the "OP" logo are trademarks belonging to Outskirts Press, Inc.

PRINTED IN THE UNITED STATES OF AMERICA

*The men who in the conflict led*
*And for the Union fought and bled*
*Tho' passing on are never dead*
*And foremost still among the Free*
*Their spirits shall by this decree*
*Lead on through all eternity*

Nash Post Card, circa 1910

# Dedication

I dedicate this book to my younger brother, Dean Roussin (1952-2013), who was taken from us much too soon. Dean, you are missed by all.

# Acknowledgements

There are many individuals who have contributed to my knowledge of the Grand Army of the Republic both in general and specific information. These include both dealers and collectors. They freely shared their knowledge and expertise with me and I will always be indebted to them. Contributors to this book include: Jan Peacock who gave me the poem, "We Drank from the Same Canteen", Vann Martin and Evertt Bowles who always allowed me to photograph their collections of G.A.R. items, Joan Radcliff, Roger and Fran Heiple for sharing their wonderful canteen collections. Others contributors include: The Horse Soldier in Gettysburg, Leonard Shippy, Todd Rittenhouse, Brad Pruden, George Finlayson, Roger Colton, Dan Mitchell and Kathie Roussin. The G.A.R. museums in Springfield, Illinois, and Philadelphia also allowed me to photograph much of their collection. I want to thank my wife, Kathie, who encouraged me and helped proofread this manuscript. Her many suggestions, while not always followed, were always appreciated. Without the help of all these people, this book would not have been written.

# Contents

**Preface** .................................................................................................................. 1
**The G.A.R.** ............................................................................................................ 2
**A Recurring Theme** ............................................................................................. 3
**We Drank From the Same Canteen** .................................................................... 5
**Canteen and Horseshoe Advertisement** ............................................................ 6
**Canteen Drops** ..................................................................................................... 7
**Pins, Ribbons, & Ribbons with Canteens** ......................................................... 9
**Badges without Ribbons** ................................................................................... 18
**Stick Pins, Watch Chains, and Fob** ................................................................. 27
**Miniature Canteens** ........................................................................................... 29
**Metal Canteens or Whiskey Flask** ................................................................... 36

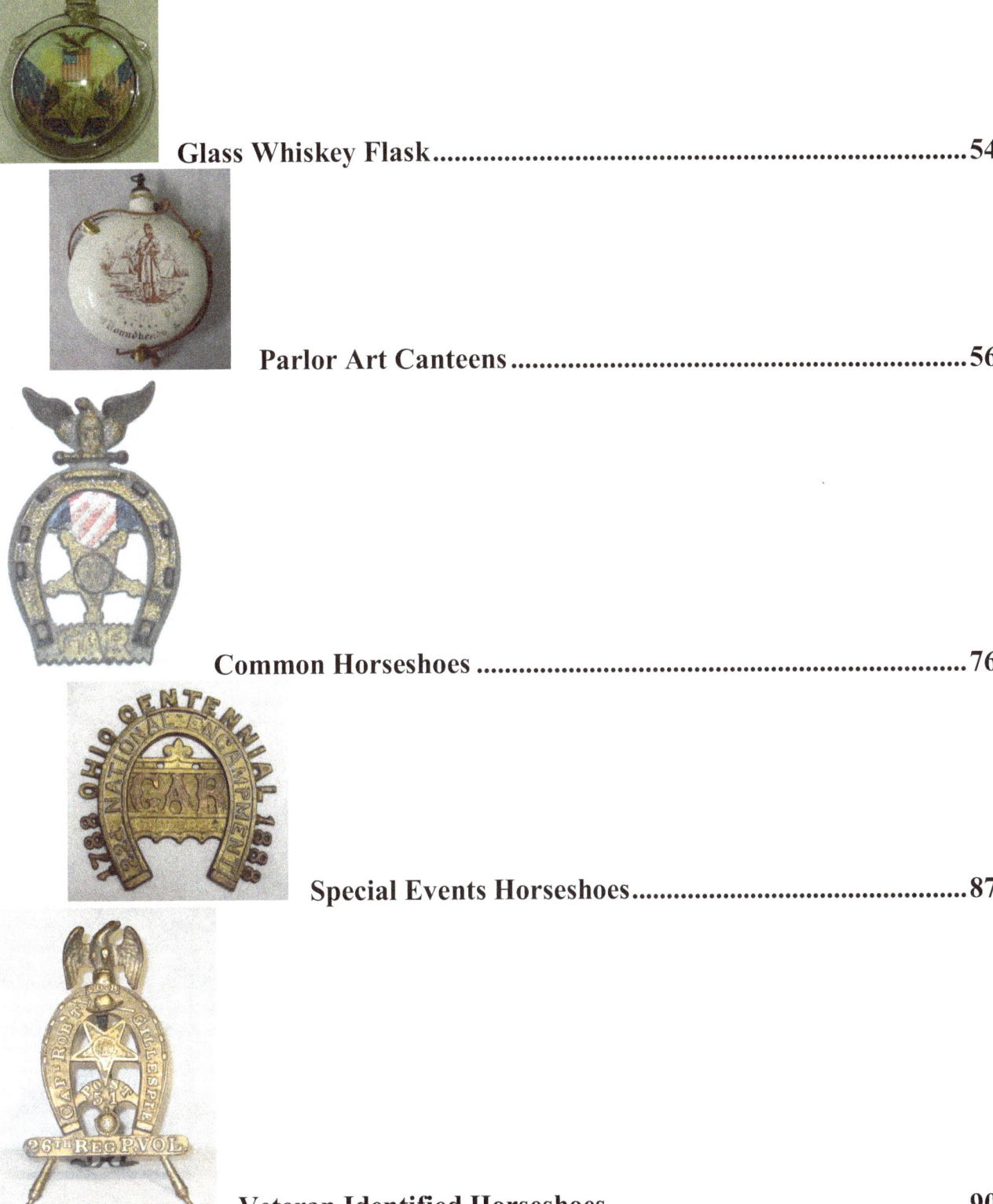

**Glass Whiskey Flask**................................................................54

**Parlor Art Canteens**................................................................56

**Common Horseshoes**..............................................................76

**Special Events Horseshoes**.....................................................87

**Veteran Identified Horseshoes**................................................90
**Appendix: List of Badge and Horseshoe Manufacturers**............96
**Bibliography**..........................................................................97

# Preface

The material contained in this work covers many examples of the use of canteen and horseshoe designs by the Grand Army of the Republic. This resource book gives the novice collector, as well as the established one, an opportunity to see and compare the many variations of souvenir canteens and horseshoes. These include canteen badges, miniatures, metal and porcelain canteens as well as the large variety of souvenir horseshoes. The collecting of Grand Army of the Republic memorabilia has become very popular over the last few decades mostly because the cost of collecting Civil War relics has become so expensive. On the other hand, the cost of Grand Army items is still very affordable and the number of items produced by them is staggering.

There have been several well written books published in the last few years on local histories of the Grand Army particularly in the area of departments or states. The authors of these books have used related ribbons, badges and other items to supplement or accent their study. But, there have been only a few books written in the field of collecting the physical regalia that the veterans left behind. The first book to tackle this field was Collecting Grand Army of the Republic Memorabilia by R. Brad Long, 1990. In this 40 pages long book, Mr. Long covered a wide range of items. Nothing more was produced on this subject until 2005, when Dennis M. Gregg produced his price guide, A Collector's Identification and Price Guide for Grand Army of the Republic Memorabilia. This guide was a general listing of memorabilia and their current values. In 2008, my first book was published, Belts, Plates, and Swords of the Grand Army of the Republic and Sons of Union Veterans of the Civil War. In this book, I attempted to narrow the collecting field down to one specific area. I was able to identify more than a hundred belts and buckles associated with the G.A.R. and S.U.V. and nearly thirty swords and their makers.

Canteens and Horseshoes, is my second endeavor at creating a collector's book on Grand Army memorabilia. The book is divided into two sections. The first section looks at the various ways that the canteen design was used by the Grand Army. Canteen designs were printed on ribbons and canteen drops were added to badges. Miniature metal canteens were produced with felt, silk, or wool covers. These were stamped with information which included posts and encampments. Larger metal canteens were produced and many times used as a whiskey flask. "Parlor Art," canteens were produced on which veterans put their name, regiment, G.A.R. post, or other information. Some Canteens were made of glass. The second section shows three types of horseshoes. The first type shows the many kinds of common or generic horseshoes. These were shoes that were produced and sold at many encampments. They usually have the letters G.A.R. or a membership badge or star added with no other information. This section is followed by the Special Events horseshoes, which had specific information added as to date or location. The final type of horseshoe, is like the "Parlor Art" canteens, was made for the individual veteran. On the horseshoe, veterans included their name, regiment, and G.A.R. post. The design varied with the branch of service. These "Parlor Art" horseshoes were large and were meant to have a prominent place in the parlor or over the fireplace. Each of these, like the porcelain canteen, are rare unto themselves. Both can be identified to an individual veteran. Each is a one of a kind.

In the appendix, I listed the manufactures whose tags and stampings appear on the canteens and horseshoes in this book. Many of these canteens and horseshoes were not marked by a manufacturer or the information has become lost. This makes it difficult to identify a particular badge to a specific manufacturer. There were probably many local concerns, which made badges and ribbons for a local event and these items were never marked.

Due to ever changing prices, this work makes no attempt to place a value on the items shown. The closest is to say that most of the memorabilia shown is still under a hundred dollars. Of course the exceptions include the Parlor Art canteens and horseshoes which have a greater value. Like Civil War relics, G.A.R. memorabilia can fluctuate widely from dealer to dealer and depending on its location.

Please remember that this collector's guide, while extensive does not reflect all the canteens and horseshoes that were made for the G.A.R. Every day a new badge or horseshoe will be pulled out of great Grandpa's trunk and will appear on the market. Happy Collecting! Douglas Roussin 2014

# The G.A.R.

In 1949, sixteen members of the greatest of all Civil War Veteran's organizations met in Indianapolis, Indiana. These frail old men were meeting for the last time. Of all the great topics they had discussed over the last 83 years, there was one last topic for discussion. This was the disbandment of their organization, the Grand Army of the Republic. They were aware that the "noblest generation" had only a little time left and it was time for them to say good-bye for the last time. They knew that in the next decade, most if not all would be gone. Indeed, by 1959, all were gone. They wondered how they would be remembered. As soldiers, they would fade into history, but they knew what they had done would be forever remembered by a grateful country. This would be enough.

The Grand Army had its beginning almost as soon as the last bullet of the Civil War had been fired. It was organized in 1866, by Dr. Benjamin F. Stephenson, who had served in the 14th Illinois infantry during the war. He, with several others felt a need to maintain contact with other veterans who had survived the last four years of Civil War. The Grand Army of the Republic was only one of several organizations which were formed after the war. Despite its shaky start, it would become the largest of all veterans groups. By 1890, its membership would climb to over 400,000 with 8,600 Posts throughout the United States plus a number in foreign countries.

The stated purpose of the Grand Army was to preserve the fraternal feeling of comradeship, to support, care for and educate soldier's orphans; to maintain their widow's well being and to assist disabled soldiers. These principles were carried out with the founding of many soldier's and orphan's homes. The aims of the Grand Army and their recommendations were adopted by the Congress of the United States in the form of many laws, pensions, and other assistances for the veterans. In 1868, the then Commander-on-Chief of the G.A.R., General John A. Logan, of Illinois, issued General Order #11. This order designated May 30, as a Memorial Day to remember the sacrifice of fallen comrades who died in the defense of their country during the Civil War. Flowers were to be placed on all graves of fallen soldiers. This became known as Decoration Day.

The Grand Army was designed as a military organization. At the local level, Posts was set up. The Posts within a state or territory formed a Department. All the Departments were subject to a National organization headed by a Commander-in-Chief. Veterans in small towns and large cities form local Posts. Generally, these Posts were named after a decreased comrade. However, some Posts were named for generals, battles, and sometimes for the name of the town where the Post was located. A few Posts had no names at all. Regardless, the same name could not be used twice within the Department.

Each Post had a Post Commander and other officers which conducted the business. The members set the schedule for meeting and other events. Once a year members of different Posts met for the Annual Department Encampment. At the Department Encampment, a Department Commander and other Department officers would be chosen and delegates selected for the National Encampment. In all, there were 83 National Encampments. The first of these was held in Indianapolis, Indiana, in 1866. Encampments were held in many locations across the country, with the final one again in Indianapolis. It was fitting that the beginning and end be at the same location.

The Annual and National Encampments were very important events and would last for many days. The National Encampment gave a great deal of prestige to the hosting city. Many events were planned. These included parades, parties, banquets and lots of speeches.

Several organizations were created or became affiliated with the G.A.R. The Sons of Union Veterans was formed in 1881. This was followed by the Women's Relief Corp, 1883, Daughter of Union Veterans, 1885, and Ladies of the G.A.R., 1886. These organizations coordinated their events many times with the G.A.R. encampments.

In summation, the G.A.R. was organized for Civil War veterans. It worked for them in obtaining pensions, veteran's homes and much more. It made the government aware of its duty to the men who had saved the Union. It was a sad moment when the last member left Indianapolis in 1949. The end of an era had come at last. But, do to their efforts, America was changed forever.

# A Recurring Theme
## (We Drank From the Same Canteen)

The Grand Army of the Republic was a unique organization. In the 83 years of its existence, the members were prolific in the amount of items that were made for them. With over 8,000 Posts, the members were allowed a large latitude on what they could acquire because there were no real guidelines on what was needed. As a result, Posts and individuals could adopt what they liked. Members were free to decorate their Posts any way they wanted and adopt uniforms and other regalia. The veterans loved medals and ribbons, and they would take every opportunity to have one made. Many large manufacturers sent out catalogs. As a result, there are literally thousands of ribbons and badges that were produced. They were produced for parades, parties, banquets, annual and national encampments. The richer and more affluent posts were having badges and ribbons made for many occasions. Special badges and ribbons were made for their delegates to the National Encampments. If you add to this the vendors who sold souvenir badges and ribbons at these events, the number produced for the G.A.R. is overwhelming.

In collecting Grand Army memorabilia, I kept running across the motto, "We Drank from the Same Canteen". It was printed on ribbons and badges. Many times a small canteen drop was added to the badge. I gave it little thought, until I noticed it on the larger metal canteens which the veteran used as a whiskey flask on many occasions. Why did the Grand Army use this saying so often? Then one day, while looking through an old Life magazine (January 6, 1961), I ran across an article which put all the pieces together. The story was entitled, <u>A Dauntless Samaritan</u>. The story was about the Battle of Fredericksburg, December, 1862. As with many Civil War battles, the Battle of Fredericksburg, was a disaster for the Union. General Ambose Burnside, in an effort to break Lee's lines, crossed into Fredericksburg and threw five divisions against the Confederate lines at the foot of Marye's Heights. Charging across open fields, the Union divisions received deadly fire from the Confederate positions behind a stone wall. By the end of the day, 13,000 men, lay dead or wounded in front of the wall. Many of the wounded, unable to be moved, lay all night in the December cold. The next day, moved by compassion for the wounded, a young soldier by the name of, Sergeant Richard Kirkland, of the 2$^{nd}$ South Carolina Volunteers asked permission to aid the wounded. Being told he could carry no weapons or a white flag, and that he was probably a dead man the

**<u>The Angel of Marye's Heights</u>**
This monument was dedicated to the memory of Sgt. Richard Kirkland for his bravery and compassion for the wounded on Marye's Heights. Kirkland in the face of the enemy was armed only with canteens. He administered to the wounded for a hour and a half to the cheers of the Union soldiers. His story does not end here. Less than a year later, the brave Kirkland was killed at the Battle of Chickamauga.

second he showed himself from behind the stone wall, he was given permission. Armed only with canteens he jumped across the wall and began to give water to the wounded. To the astonishment of his comrades, the Union soldiers held their fire. A cheer went up from the Union lines and for an hour and a half no shot was fired as he cared for the wounded.

This story seemed to bring home why the Grand Army used the canteen and the motto so often on their ribbons and badges. To the veteran, the canteen was a reminder of the long marches, thirst in the heat of battle, and sharing water with the wounded. The image of the canteen represented to the Grand Army the comradeship the veterans felt for each other.
.
In the following pages, "We Drank from the Same Canteen", will occur over and over again on ribbons and badges as well as on miniature and large metal canteens. This motto will be found on one of the parlor art canteens as well.

# "WE DRANK FROM THE SAME CANTEEN"

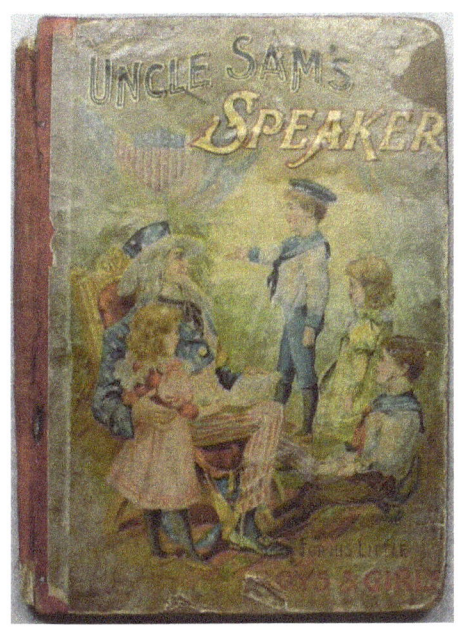

There are bonds of all sorts in this world of ours,
Fetters of friendship and ties of flowers,
And true lovers' knots, I ween!
The girl and the boy are bound by a kiss,
But there's never a bond, old friend, like this
We have drunk from the same canteen!

It was sometimes water, and sometimes milk,
And sometimes applejack, fine as silk;
But, whatever the tipple has been,
We shared it together, in bane or bliss,
And I warm to you, friend, when I think of this:
We have drunk from the same canteen!

The rich and the great sit down to dine,
And they quaff to each other in sparkling wine,
From glasses of crystal and green;
But I guess in their golden potations they miss
The warmth of regard to be found in this-
We have drunk from the same canteen!

We have shared our blankets and tents together,
We have marched and fought in all kinds of weather,
And hungry and full we have been;
Had days of battle and days of rest;
But this memory I cling to and love the best-
We have drunk from the came canteen!

For, when wounded I lay on the outer slope,
With my blood flowing fast and but little hope
Upon which faint spirit could lean;
Oh, then, I remember, you crawled to my side,
And, bleeding so fast it seemed both must have died,
We drank from the same canteen!

"We Drank from the Same Canteen", was a reoccurring theme of the Grand Army of the Republic. This poem is found in the children's book, "Uncle Sam's Speaker, For His Little Boys and Girls", circa 1920. This book belonged to Miss Florence Ethel MacDonald which bares her name and the date 1921, on the inside cover. The book is filled with poems for religious and patriotic holidays.
Book Courtesy: Jan Peacock

# Advertisement

While canteens and horseshoes were used in a variety of ways by the Grand Army, it is rare to see their design used to advertise a product or event. Below, are two examples that used the horseshoe and canteen for advertising purposes.

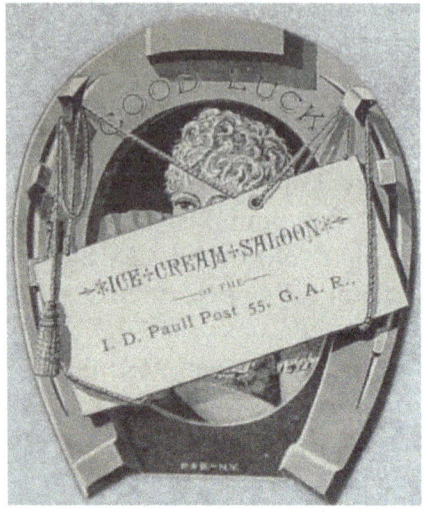

### Menu on back of card

*ICES*
Lemon, 15 cents   Strawberry, 15 cents
Vanilla, 15 cents   Chocolate, 15 cents
Harlequin, 15 cents
Orange Sherbets, 20 cents
Strawberries and Cream, 30 cents
Fruit
Grapes, Oranges, Pine Apples, Bananas
Coffee, 10 cents   Tea 10 cents
Soda with Fruit Syrups, 10 cents
Lemonade, 10 cents

This small advertising menu in the shape of a horseshoe has no date or location as to when or where it took place. It is simply marked, I. D. Paull Post 55, G.A.R. The menu could have been made for a summer social evening the Post had or the veterans may have manned a booth at a local fair and used the profits as part of a fund raising activity. Note the term "ICES" when referring to flavors. The prices featured on the back were not too bad.

## Schlitz Brewing Company

In 1889, the National Encampment was held in Milwaukee, Wisconsin, which was home to the Jos. Schlitz Brewing Company. To take advantage of the large number of veterans attending, the company produced a song book with a picture of a canteen on front and back. A large membership badge appears on the front with the words, "dedicated to the G.A.R. on the occasion of its 23rd Encampment at Milwaukee". On the back is written, "With compliments of the Jos. Schlitz Brewing Company, Milwaukee, Wis.". Inside the book are "War Songs of the Nation", with patriotic pictures. Each song had a special verse which was intended to increase the drinking of Schlitz Beer. I bet it worked!

# CANTEEN DROPS

A canteen drop is that part of the badge which was at one time attached to a ribbon or pin bar. Sometimes the drop was accented with a silk or cotton ribbon. On this was stamped information such as Annual and National Encampments, Soldiers and Sailors Associations or the name and location of a Post. These ribbons could be solid in color or a combination of colors: red, white, and blue. Over the course of time and due to the fragile nature of many ribbons and badges, the drop has detached itself from the ribbon or bar, but, has survived on its own. As many canteen drops were non-descript and were used over the years for different events, it is now nearly impossible to connect them to any particular event. On the other hand, some canteen drops did have specific information to a singular event. This allows other examples to be found which are still intact. Once the original badge has been found, it is sometimes possible to purchase the missing part and replacement ribbon. This has allowed many collectors the opportunity to reunite the parts and put the badge back together. Below are examples of canteens drops which were once attached to a badge or ribbon. These drops show a wide range of designs.

### Gilt Canteen with U. S.
This gilt canteen measures only 1 inch tall. It is stamped with U. S. on one side. A fine chain or wire once held this canteen to a ribbon or bar clasp. This canteen is hollow and shows a seam along the edge.

**Nickel Canteen Drop**: This drop is a little larger at 1 ¼ inches. It is made in two pieces which are held together with three loops. These hold a twisted wire. In the center of the canteen are intertwined G.A.R. letters within a circle. This is surrounded by the motto: "We drank from the same canteen, 1861-1866". The design appears on both sides of the canteen.

**Solid Canteen Drop:** This small solid canteen is 1 inch tall with nickel plate. On one side is the word Gettysburg and on the other appear the letters U. S. The word "Gettysburg" suggest it was made for one of the encampments which were held at that location. It is possible that this was just a souvenir badge sold to the tourist who visited this battlefield.

**33rd National Encampment** This canteen design appears to have been made for many years for a variety of events. The canteen measures 1 ½ inches tall. This drop was made for the 33rd National Encampment, Sept. 4-9, 1899, in Philadelphia. On the front is stamped Independence Hall with large G.A.R. letters surrounding a dome. A stamped wire rope goes around the canteen and would be attached to the pin bar. These canteen drops seldom had a ribbon. They were a stock design which could be stamped for any occasion. On the reverse of this canteen is marked, "Schwaab S & S. Co., Milwaukee, Pat. Appl'd For".

**32nd Nat'l Encampment** Here is another drop made by the Schwaab Company. It was made for the 32nd National Encampment which was held in Cincinnati, Ohio, on September 5-10, 1898. In the center of the canteen is a raised membership star of the Grand Army. This drop has lost all of its gilt and has much pitting

## 26th Encampment

This hard rubber drop often referred to as gutta percha, was made for the 26th National Encampment in Washington, D.C., 1892. The information appears on one side. The other side has, "Grand Army of the Republic, 1861-Veteran-1866". This particular drop is black, but, others are found in a brown tone.

8

# Pins & Printed Ribbons

Thousands of ribbons were created for the Grand Army, but very few used the canteen design. This brings up the question of why there were so many canteen badges and so few ribbons with canteens.

A ribbon is a piece of cloth with printing on it which announces a particular event or supplies other information. The ribbon is stamped in ink and can be found in a variety of colors and combinations.

Above are a set of three pins that were made and distributed at many events. These are generic in design. They were given out at banquets and also to children and adults during parades. These paper pins were inexpensive to make. Thousands of these have survived. The first pin has a soldiers and sailor with the motto of Fraternity, Charity and Loyalty. The middle pin has a canteen with the intertwined G.A.R. letters and the motto, "We Drank from the Same Canteen" and "Welcome Comrades". The third one has the membership badge of the Grand Army.

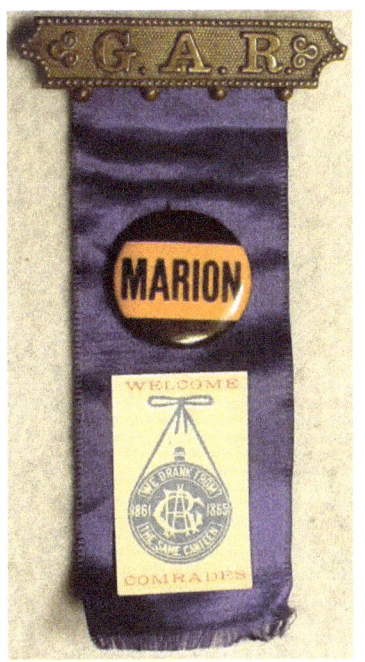

### Marion (Ohio)
The ribbon on the left is unusual in its appearance. At the top, a brass pin bar shows the letters G.A.R. A 5 ½ inch dark blue ribbon is attached with no stamping. On the ribbon is glued a paper canteen with "Welcome Comrades". This is the same parade pin that appears above. A black and orange button is attached in the center with the word Marion. This button was made by the Phila. Badge Co. The badge was probably designed for a local event by a Post with limited resources.

### Southern Illinois Soldiers Association
This bright red ribbon is 8 inches long. It was made for the "Southern Illinois Soldiers Associations--Annual Reunion--September 8, 9, & 10th, 1885," in Centralia. It has a stamped eagle and canteen with the number 3 representing the Post. The motto, "We Drank from the Same Canteen--1861-1865", appears around the Post number. The design has faded making it hard to read.

### Ogle Co. Soldiers & Sailors

Left:  This blue ribbon is 6 inch long.  It was made for the "1st Reunion--Ogle County Soldiers & Sailors Association--Oregon, Illinois--August 17 & 18, 1886".  The ribbon has a badge printed on it with an eagle holding a canteen.  There was several brass pins produced at this time on which this ribbon was patterned.  The dates 1861 and 1886 appear at the top and bottom.  The date 1861 represents the start of the Civil War and 1886 is the date the reunion.

### Southwestern Wisconsin Veteran Association

Right:  The red ribbon on the right is 8 inches long and was made for the "Fifth Annual Reunion of the Southwestern Wisconsin Veteran Associa'n".  It features the eagle holding a canteen with the Motto, "We Drank from the Same Canteen".  With age, this ribbon has faded.  The reunion was held in Darlington, Wisconsin, June 11 & 12, 1884.

### De Kalb County Camp-Fire Association

Left:  The light blue ribbon on the left has the eagle and canteen badge printed on the front.  This ribbon was made for the "4th Annual Reunion, De Kalb County Camp-Fire Association.  The ribbon has a swallow tail.  This reunion was held in Kingston, Illinois, August 22-23, 1888.

## Ribbons with Canteen Drops

This type of badge, used a miniature metal canteen with a ribbon. The ribbon could be used as a background to accent the canteen. It, also, might be used as an integral part of the badge which connected the canteen to a pin bar. The badge could contain information on the ribbon, but in most cases the information is found on the pin bar or stamped into the canteen. These badges are many times a generic badge which would be sold at any event. They were also made for specific encampments and showed this information. Of the 83 National Encampments held by the G.A.R., there was only one with a canteen incorporated into its design. This was the 40th National Encampment in 1906. This was held in Minneapolis.

## 24th National Encampment 1890

**Left:** This gold ribbon was made for the 24th National Encampment of the G. A. R. which was held in Boston in 1890. It is unusual in the number of drops that are attached to it. In the middle, is a miniature cup and plate. Below this is a tin canteen. The ribbon is stamped with a haversack which has the word "Rations". A straight pin was used to attach this ribbon to a uniform. It may have originally had a pin bar at the top.

## 28th National Encampment 1894

**Right:** This canteen ribbon was made as a souvenir for the 28th National Encampment. It was held in Pittsburgh in 1894. The pin bar has the word souvenir and from this hangs a red, white, and blue ribbon. The blue stripe has completely faded. Tied to the ribbon is a brass bar where a canteen hangs from a gold wire. The canteen has intertwined G. A. R. letters in the center and the motto, "We Drank from the Same Canteen". This emblem appears on both sides. On the back, the date 1883, is stamped and is probably the date of manufacture. The bottom part of the ribbon has unraveled. The date 1894 is almost lost.

### Flags & Canteens

Both of these badges have a canteen drop attached to American flag ribbons. This was accomplished by the use of a small tack though the flag. Both canteen drops are made of brass, but, one has a nickel finish. These canteens have the intertwined G.A.R. and the motto, "We Drank from the Same Canteen". Each badge has a different style of eagle. The badge on the left has the word souvenir on the bar under the eagle. The blue field and stars of the flags appear on different sides of the ribbon. Both flags have a swallow tail.

### Hat & Sword

The nickel pin bar is in the design of a hat and sword. Below this is a canteen with a gold color strap. On the canteen are the intertwined G.A.R. letters surrounded by the motto, "We Drank from the Same Canteen". This appears on both sides of the canteen drop. The unusual feature of this badge is the way the canteen drop has been attached to the red, white, and blue ribbon. It is attached with a small tack. Here is an example of a badge that has not generally survived very well. The canteen on a deteriorating ribbon will detach itself and become lost. This ribbon shows signs of deterioration near the top. It has a swallow tail which is unraveling.

### 25th Annual Encampment, 1891

This canteen badge was made for the 25th Annual Encampment, held in Pennsylvania, February, 1891. The pin bar shows that date. In the center of the pin bar is a circle with a "Key Stone", the symbol of Pennsylvania. On the key stone are the letters G.A.R. A red ribbon connects the pin bar to the rest of the badge. An unusual feature of this badge is the ribbon. It is a replacement from another badge. Because, printed on the inside of the ribbon is Pittsburg, 1894. On the canteen appears a campfire scene with a cooking pot. This design first appeared on the back of the 1886 membership badge (Type 5). Around the campfire is the inscription, 25th Annual Encampment, Dept. Pa. The back of the canteen is inscribed, "Presented by Post 62 (Lieut. S.C. Potts Post) and 468 (Fred C. Ward Post), Altoona, Pa.". These two Altoona Posts jointly hosted this encampment and had the badge made for this occasion.

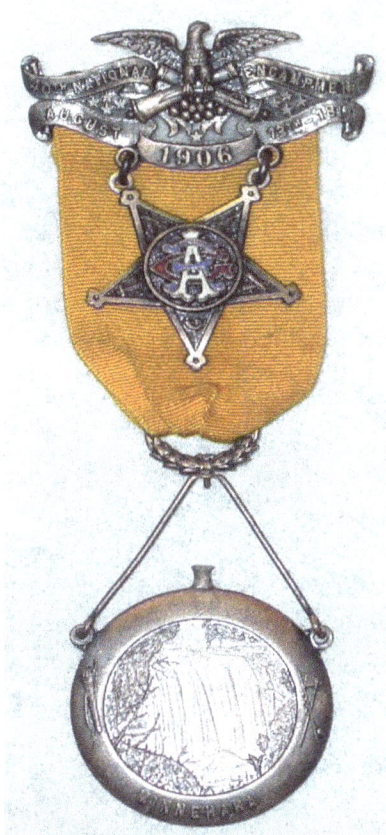

### 40 National Encampment 1906

This is the only National Encampment badge to use the canteen design. The 40th National Encampment was held, Aug. 13-18, 1906, in Minneapolis. The badge has the membership eagle at the top surrounded by the Encampment information and date. Hanging from the pin bar is the membership star with intertwined G.A.R. letters. These letters are red, white, and blue enamel. A gold ribbon connects the pin bar to a wreath which holds the canteen. An unusual feature is the way that the canteen has been attached to the wreath. It is fastened on a swivel, which allows the canteen to rotate. On one side of the canteen is a picture of a large building with a tower. Around the top rim the word "Member" is inscribed and "G.A.R. memorial Halls, Minneapolis".

Many encampment badges have local landmarks incorporated in their design. On the back of this canteen, a picture of a waterfall can be seen with the word, "Minnehaha". A bow and arrow and crossed tomahawks are on the side. The manufacturer of this badge is "S. D. Childs & Co., engravers, Chicago".

### Dept. of Wash. & Alaska

**Left:** The badge on the left was made for the 1902 Encampment held in Everett, Wash. The pin bar has Everett, 1902, followed by a red, white, and blue ribbon. The ribbon is an integral part of the badge and holds a gilt drop. The canteen has G.A.R. letters which are intertwined and surrounded by a wreath. Below the wreath is the motto, "We Drank from the Same Canteen". The date, June 24-27 separates the words Encampment and Dept. of Washington and Alaska. The reverse of the canteen is stamped, "Schwaab S. & S. Co., Milwaukee". This company produced a large number of canteen badges of this design. The canteen was a stock piece which could be easily stamped and is found with numerous designs and dates. Many times this canteen was made without a ribbon.

### Department of New York-Annual Encampment

**Above Right**: This beautiful badge is dated 1910. It is a delegate badge to the 44th Annual Encampment, Dept. of New York. The enameling of badges was very popular at the turn of the century and the badge reflects this. At the top of the badge is an eagle with spread wings. He is holding a ribbon in his claws which says Syracuse, June, 1910. Below this is the complete membership badge of the G.A.R., the three length chain connect the drops. The middle drop has, "Delegate, 44th Annual Encampment, Dept. of New York with G.A.R. letters. The canteen is marked U.S. The entire badge is accented with a red ribbon.

### 8th District

The pin bar to this badge has a paper tag at the top with the word souvenir. Many times this type of bar would have the veteran's name or other information printed on it. The pin bar holds a red, white, and blue ribbon which has gold stamping. The ribbon says, "The Reunion of the Veterans of the 8th Congressional District, Sept. 17, 1907, Muncie, Ind.". From the ribbon hangs a circular tin disk with a picture of a canteen. The reverse is stamped, "Whitehead & Hoag Co., Newark, N.J.

### Guest Badge Trenton, N. J.

This large badge was made for a guest of the 1905 Annual Reunion and was held in Trenton, New Jersey. The top pin bar has the word GUEST printed on white celluloid. From this pin bar hangs a long black ribbon. A white porcelain canteen is attached to the pin bar by a chain. Printed in gold script on the canteen are the words, "Annual Reunion, Grand Army of the Republic, June 22-23, 1905, Trenton, N. J.". The large porcelain canteen is an unusual feature for G.A.R. badges. Though several examples are known to exist, they are quite rare.

### Washington, 1892

This badge has a large 2 inch canteen drop. It is the largest canteen drop produced for the Grand Army. On the canteen are the several branches of service: infantry, artillery, navy, and cavalry. In the center of the canteen is the emblem for the G.A.R. The canteen is held to the pin bar by a small chain on either side. On the pin bar are the letters G.A.R. across an American Flag with the insignia of the branches of service. Accenting the badge is a red, white, and blue ribbon. Printed on the ribbon in gold letters are, "26th Annual Encampment, G.A.R., Washington, D.C., Sept. 1892". Sometimes, this badge can be found on ribbons with no stamping.

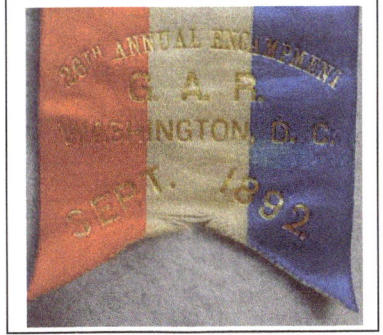

15

## 24TH Annual Encampment

This Souvenir badge was made for the 24th Annual Encampment, but, which one? This badge has no other information. The pin bar simply has G.A.R. A 1 ½ inch chain holds a large 2 inch canteen drop. On it is stamped 24th Annual Encampment and the word souvenir at the bottom. The center has the soldier and sailor emblem surrounded by "Grand Army of the Republic-1861-1866 and Veteran". The emblem is on top of crossed cannons and rifles and it has a sword and cannon balls. These emblems represent 3 of the 4 branches of service. Accenting the badge is a deteriorating swallow tailed red, white, and blue ribbon. The condition of the ribbon is reflecting its age. The second badge is similar and was probably made by the same company that produced the previous badge. The pin bar is stamped brass and has the 4 branches of service with an American flag and G. A. R. letters. Two chains of different length, holds the 2 inch canteen at a slight tilt. On this canteen appear the 4 branches of service with the soldier and sailor emblem in the middle. A red, white, and blue ribbon accents this piece.

### 11th Michigan Cavalry

This badge was made for the 12th Annual Reunion of the 11th Michigan Cavalry. The reunion was held in Quincy, Michigan, Oct. 18, 1897. Quincy is stamped on the pin bar and from this hangs the standard Schwaab S & S. Co. canteen. The Schwaab Company was located in Milwaukee. In the center of the canteen are the intertwined G.A.R. letters surrounded by a wreath. Around this is stamped the date and other information. A tattered yellow-gold ribbon accents this badge. This is the color of the cavalry and probably why it was chosen. If other badges of this design had ribbons, they must have become easily detached.

16

### 29th National Encampment 1895

These badges were designed for the 29th National Encampment which was held in Louisville, 1895. The pin bars are fan shaped. On one are swords, and on the other rifles. Hanging from this is a small canteen which says, "29th Nat'l Encampment--Louisville". In the center are intertwined G. A. R. letters. A red ribbon accents the first badge while a blue ribbon hangs from the second. The makers are "Heeren Bros. & Co.". This is stamped on the back of the canteen. Under the maker's name are cross cannon. The cross cannon indicates that the brass came from Civil War surplus cannon. These badges are examples of how the badge companies targeted the different branches of service. There is probably a similar badge for artillery.

### Chattanooga/Chickamauga

This souvenir badge was made to commemorate the battle of Chickamauga. It was probably sold between 1895 and 1913 to tourist visiting the park and at the 1913 joint reunion of the blue and gray. The canteen has a picture of the Snodgrass House with two cannon. The canteen is held to the pin bar by a chain connected to a red and white ribbon. A second longer white ribbon accents this. The only other information is located on the pin bar. It has the word Chattanooga.
Courtesy: Vann R. Martin

## Badges Without Ribbons

The common canteen badge is one that might have been ordered by any Post and were given out or sold at many events. These badges have no specific information as to a certain time or event, but would have general information or symbols. The symbols might include intertwined G.A.R. letters, a membership eagle or star, and the motto, "We Drank from the Same Canteen". Many times these were stock badges which a company kept on hand and could be sold and shipped very quickly. Some Post used them for fundraising. They were also used as generic souvenirs at Annual and National Encampments.

### Amputee Badge
This badge is made of stamped tin. The membership eagle has a gold color. It has a long hook on the back which holds a large 1 ½ inch canteen. On front of the badge is a veteran, in hat and uniform, who has lost his left arm. He is holding a flag. Around the edge is the Motto "We Drank from the Same Canteen". A membership star in high relief is on the back which has a gold color. Around the star is printed, "Grand Army of the Republic, 1861-veteran-1866. The two halves of the canteen have been soldered together.

### Ladies Canteen
The eagle on this badge is nickel on stamped brass. A large brass loop holds the canteen chain. The canteen is brass and quite ornate. A flower and vine pattern appears on both sides. A strip of brass encircles the edge of the canteen. The canteen stopper was designed to be removed. This badge is very feminine for a veterans' piece. It was probably sold to the members of one of the affiliated organizations such as the Ladies of the G.A.R., Daughters of Union Veterans, or the Women's Relief Corp. It is possible that this canteen, at one time, contained perfume or smelling salts.

### Ohio Buckeye
This unique badge was made for one of the Annual Encampments of the Department of Ohio (The Buckeye State). The badge has a gilt eagle pin bar. The shield which has been glued on is colored paper. The canteen is attached to the eagle by a braided string. The canteen itself is made from a buckeye which has been cut in half and put back together to form the canteen. A small brass spout was inserted at the top.

### Simple Canteen Badge
This simple badge, made of stamped brass has the eagle on top. The canteen is attached to the eagle with a small twisted wire. The canteen measures a little over an inch. It has the intertwined G.A.R. letters and the dates 1861 and 1865. These stock pieces were probably sold at many events. The badge design was also stamped on many Soldiers and Sailors association ribbons.

### Artillery Canteen
This badge was targeted for a veteran who had served in the Artillery branch of service. It is very simple in its design. At the top are crossed cannon. Attached to this is a one inch brass canteen with the letters U. S. Because of the generic nature of this badge, it is hard to associate it with the G.A.R. This badge could be related to other organizations or military groups.

## Schwaab Stamp & Seal Co.

Andrew Schwaab was born in New York in 1853. His family moved to Milwaukee when he was a boy. He founded the Northwestern Stamp Company in 1881 and it grew with branches in Chicago and St. Paul. He later sold these branches and consolidated the company in Milwaukee. In 1888, he changed the name of his company to Schwaab Stamp and Seal Company. He operated this until his death in 1911. During this time, he acquired several companies including an engraving company. The Schwaab Company made badges for the Grand Army and numerous other organizations. This company has remained in the Schwaab family and is still in operation. Today, the company operates under the name of Schwaab, Inc. Source: Schwaab Inc. website.

Above are three Annual Encampment badges made by the Schwaab Stamp & Seal Company. The pin bars have the word souvenir printed in large letters. Hanging from this is a canteen. On the canteen is printed Annual State Encampment. It has the intertwined G.A.R. letters in a wreath. Below the wreath is the motto, "We Drank from the Same Canteen". The first canteen has no date and was a generic piece while the others are dated 1896 and 1897. The pin bar and canteen are stock pieces and could be stamped with numerous designs and dates.

### 31st National Encampment
This badge was made in 1897, for the 31st National Encampment which was held in Buffalo, New York. More than a thousand delegates attended this Encampment. This Schwaab badge has the pin bar and canteen. The canteen is stamped 31st National Encampment, Buffalo, N.Y. Aug. 23-28, 1897. It has the intertwined GA.R. encircled by a wreath.

| 30th National Encampment 1896 | Decoration Day 1900 | Vicksburg Jubilee 1917 |

These badges represent the diversity of designs and occasions that are found on badges made by Schwaab.

**30th National Encampment-1896:** The first badge was made for the St. Paul National Encampment held in 1896. 1,122 delegates attended this Encampment. The badge has the membership star of the G.A.R. in the center and is surrounded by other information.

**Decoration Day-1900:** Decoration Day was founded by the G.A.R. This badge has intertwined G.A.R. letters surrounded by a wreath. The inscription states, "Decoration Day at Marvin Preston's". Who or what is Marvin Preston? It sounds like an exclusive bar or restaurant. In small letters below the wreath is the motto, "We Drank from the Same Canteen".

**Vicksburg Jubilee-1917:** This badge was made for the Federal & Confederate Peace Jubilee which was held in Vicksburg, October, 1917. The main design of this badge is a dove with an olive branch in its mouth. The dove is surrounded by a wreath. Thousands attended this event. Many banquets, speeches, battlefield tours were held. There was even a large parade.

### Sons of Veterans
These souvenir badges were made for The Sons of Union Veterans of the United States of America, (today known as The Sons of Union Veterans of the Civil War). The S.U.V. was established in 1881 as an auxiliary to the G.A.R. Each canteen has Annual Encampment, Sons of Veterans printed on it. No dates are given. Many times the Son's Encampments were held in conjunction with G.A.R. encampments. The badge has the insignia of the S.U.V. These were probably stock pieces and sold on many occasions. Note the difference of the pin bars between the two badges.

### Shiloh Survivors

This is a rare two sided gilt badge for The National Association of Battle of Shiloh Survivors. Later versions of this badge are blank on the back. This variation has the log on top with the word Shiloh. Hanging from this is a coffee tin. The canteen has the motto, "We Now Drink from the Same Canteen". In the center is a federal shield with two soldiers holding a flag. The shield is surrounded by rifles, cannons, tents, sabers and has the infantry insignia. The reverse has a battle scene, with gunboats and artillery. "The National Association of Battle of Shiloh Survivors" appears around the edge. Courtesy: Vann R. Martin

The formation of the Shiloh Survivors was patterned after the G. A. R. It was formed in Denver, 1905. The object of this association was to perpetuate memories, collect data, and to nurture fraternal feeling among those who participated. This would be though meetings, discussions related to personal incidents, and personal functions. It was open to all soldiers, sailors, and marines who had participated in the battle. The original membership dues were fifty cents. Annual and National Encampments were to be held at the same time and place as the G.A.R. Encampments and Associations could be formed in each G.A.R. Department.

### Illinois Post & Department

These simple bronze colored badges were designed and made for the Department of Illinois. One was adopted by a Chicago Post as its official badge. The first badge has a pin bar showing Post information. This badge was made for U. S. Grant Post #28 and was located in Chicago. The drop canteen has the portrait of General Grant. A red ribbon once accented this piece and traces of it are still found on the back. The Department badge has a rectangular pin bar with 1861-1865. The canteen drop has the portrait of General Grant surrounded by the words: "Dept. of Illinois" and the letters G.A.R.

**Washington, D.C.**

This badge was made for one of the Annual or National Encampments held in Washington, D.C. The exact one is unknown as no date is given. The badge shows the Capitol building with crossed cannon. As no other branch of service is shown, this badge was probably targeted to a veteran who had served in the artillery during the war maybe in the defense of Washington. The canteen drop has G. A. R. and Washington D.C.

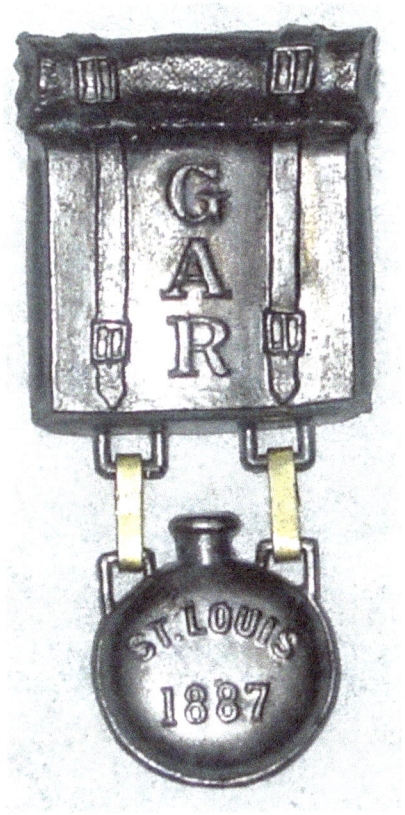

**St. Louis & Chicago**

These two badges use the knapsack and canteen design. The knapsack and blanket pin bar is a stock piece which could be used for many events. The knapsack on the left has the letters G.A.R. and the other has a kepi on it. The canteen drop was easily stamped and attached to the knapsack. The first is stamped St. Louis and the other Chicago. Both have the date 1887. The National Encampment was held in St. Louis in 1887. It is unclear if these are related to this event.

23

### Recycled Badge
This badge was made from recycled parts. It is a generic badge with no date or information. The large membership star has two holes at the top. This indicates that the star was made for another larger badge and these holes connected the star to the rest of the badge. A small pin is soldered to the back. A canteen drop was then added to finish the badge design. This canteen was used on many badges. The maker of this badge is unknown.

### Chief Anderson
This badge was made by the Whitehead & Hoag, Co. of Newark, N. J., for one or more of the Indiana Encampments. This badge is made of celluloid. It has the G.A.R. membership badge on one side and a portrait of Chief Anderson on the other. He was a famous Delaware Indian who was born in Pennsylvania and moved to Indiana. Always at peace with the white man, Anderson, Indiana, was named in his honor. This canteen can be found attached to a tie clip which was also sold at Indiana Encampments.

### 28th National Encampment
This badge was made for the 28th National Encampment which was held in Pittsburg, Pa., 1894. 1,153 delegates attended this Encampment. A sword is used as the pin bar from which hangs a small canteen. In the center of the canteen are intertwined G.A.R. letters. Surrounding the letters is "28th Nat. Encampment, Pittsburg". This badge was made by Heeren Bros. & Co., Pittsburg, Pa. They used a similar design for other encampments.

### 30th National Encampment
This souvenir sword and canteen badge was made for the 30th Nat'l Encampment in St. Paul, Minn., 1896. The pin bar is in the shape of an Officer's sword. Hanging from this is a canteen with the intertwined G.A.R. letters in the center and other information is around the edge. This badge is stamped, "Heeren Bros. & Co., Pittsburg, Pa."

### Boston and Buffalo
**Boston:** This is a small badge. The pin bar has GAR on black enamel. Both the pin bar and canteen are trimmed in gilt. On the canteen is inscribed Boston, 1890.
**Buffalo:** The buffalo canteen is probably only part of a badge. The rank bar does not have a pin. It has two pieces of brass which holds the ribbon. The badge has a Post Officer's rank strap. The two bars indicate the rank of "Officer of the Day". Tied to the strap is a ribbon holding a canteen which reads "Buffalo, 1897". It has intertwined G.A.R. letters.

### Gettysburg & Veteran
These badges are simple in design. The Gettysburg badge has an eagle as a pin bar and a gilt canteen with the word Gettysburg. This was probably a souvenir badge from an encampment or a badge sold at one of the souvenir shops in Gettysburg. The second badge has veteran on the pin bar. The canteen has the letters N.G.S.M. This is believed to stand for the National Guard of Minnesota.

25

### Flag, Button, and Canteen
The canteen badge on the left incorporates an American Flag ribbon with a Civil War Button. This is used as a pin bar. The canteen drop is held to the ribbon by twisted wire. On the canteen are the intertwined G.A.R. letters and the dates 1861-1865. Courtesy: George M. Rees

### Sweetheart Badge
This sweetheart badge was probably sold at one of the Gettysburg Encampments. But, it may have been a souvenir sold at one of the many shops. It has a metal pin bar ribbon. From this hangs the small metal gilt canteen with the word Gettysburg.

### Old Canteen
These badges are quite generic in design. The pin bar simply states, "Old Canteen", and has a small canteen drop with 1861.

### Tie Clip
This tie clip canteen is made of celluloid. On one side is the portrait of Chief Anderson, a famous Delaware Indian (ca. 1755-1831). He was born in Pennsylvania and relocated to Indiana as a young man. Anderson became Chief of the Turkey clan. Always at peace with the white man, the city of Anderson, Indiana, was named for him. The other side of the canteen has the G.A.R. membership badge. This tie clip was probably sold as a souvenir at one of the Indiana Encampments. The Maker is Whitehead & Hoag Co. Newark, N. J.

## Pins, Watch Chains & Fob

### N.J.N.G. Encampment
This stick pin, while not G.A.R., shows the use of the canteen design by other military organizations. The eagle is holding a canteen with a soldier in the center. This encampment was held in Sea Girt, N. J., 1908.

### G.A.R. Stick Pin
The G.A.R. stick pin, on the right, was produced for the 1908, 42nd National Encampment which was held in Toledo, Ohio. It has the eagle holding the canteen with intertwined letters in the center. On the back is the Lord's Prayer.

### Watch Chains
**Left:** This unusual watch chain was a souvenir of the 31st National Encampment. The Encampment was held in Buffalo, New York, August 23-28, 1897. The center of the canteen has intertwined G. A. R. letters surrounded by a wreath with other information. The chain was made by the Schwaab Stamp & Seal Co., Milwaukee. The watch chain had a matching souvenir badge.

**Right:** Double chains were used to make the watch chain on the right. A canteen with the letters U. S. is attached. No other markings are found on the chain.

### Watch Fob
This watch fob measures over 6 inches in length. The ribbon is black and has a swallow tail design. A hook at the top held a watch. The ring in the center holds a small canteen. On the canteen is U.S. All metal parts have gilt. Near the top, the veteran has attached a thin gold and enamel membership pin.

## Memoriam, George Tobey Anthony

This is a memorial badge for the 7th Governor of Kansas, George Anthony, (1824-1896). Anthony was born in New York and in 1862, he organized and became Captain of the 17th New York Independent Battery of Light Artillery. After the war, he settled in Kansas and became editor of several newspapers. Anthony was elected Governor of Kansas in 1876. This badge, with his portrait, was made after his death in 1896. Hanging from his portrait is a canteen with the membership star of the G.A.R. A straight pin is attached on the back.

## Washington, 1892

This ribbon was sold as a souvenir badge at the 1892 National Encampment. The red ribbon is stamped with Washington, D. C. A stamped metal flag appears on the top and is used as a pin bar. A French liberty cap is on top of the flagpole. Hanging on a chain from the flag is a stamped canteen with the membership star and the dates 61 and 65. The letters G.A.R. also appear on the canteen.

## Coffee Cup

This small coffee cup has the membership badge and dates, 1861-1865. Around the badge is the motto, "We Drank from the Same Canteen". This cup was probably sold at one of the National Encampments.

## Miniature Canteens

The miniature souvenir canteens were sold at many encampments and were made for a large variety of groups. These groups included the Grand Army and many Soldiers and Sailors Societies and Associations, along with other reunion groups. Some Posts had special canteens made. On these were found the name of the Post and other pertinent information. Miniature canteens are about 2 ¼ inches across while some are as large as 3 inches. They were not designed to hold any kind of liquid. Miniature canteens were simply souvenirs of an event. The canteens were made of tin and sometimes were embossed. Most times, the canteen was covered with felt, wool, or silk. These coverings were stamped with information. The stamping could have lettering of silver or gold. The coverings on most miniatures did not survive very well. They are found with moth holes and much of the lettering has faded. This makes it very hard to read. But, occasionally, one is found in pristine condition.

**Common Canteens**
These are two common souvenir canteens. The first measures 2 ¼ inches across. This canteen usually has a felt or wool covering. But, this miniature has been painted yellow. No other markings are found. The second is a small copper canteen. No information is found on this canteen.

**Logan Canteen**
This tin canteen has the bust of Civil War General John A. Logan. Logan was one of the founders of the G.A.R. The reverse has, "We Drank from the Same Canteen/ GAR/Souvenir". A red, white and blue cord is attached.

General Logan (1826-1886) was a lawyer, Illinois politician, and Civil War general. As one of the founders of the Grand Army, he was elected Commander in Chief three times (1869-1870-1871). It is possible that this canteen was a part of his political campaign for Vice President in 1884. He unsuccessfully ran for that office on the James G. Blaine, Republican ticket. He died two years later. It is possible that this canteen was sold after his death at encampments as a memorial to him. It is impossible to determine its use as the canteen has no date.

**Slocum Post Canteen**

This canteen measures 2 ¾ inches across. This dark colored canteen is made of tin. Embossed on the center of the canteen is the G.A.R. monogram. Surrounding the monogram is, "Slocum Post No. 10 and Grand Bivouac 1886". This appears on both sides of the canteen. Slocum Post was located in Providence, Rhode Island. A wide white canvas ribbon goes though three loops on the canteen. A chain connects the canteen to a cork stopper.

### 42nd National Encampment

This canteen measures not quite 2 ½ inches. It was made for the 42nd National Encampment which was held in Toledo, Ohio, 1908. The canteen is red on one side and blue on the other. Both sides are stamped, "42nd Nat'l Encampment-Toledo, O.-Sept. 1908". Over 1,500 delegates attended this Encampment.

### Common Red Canteen

The red canteen, on the right, was sold at many events. It is 2 ½ inches across and covered with red felt or wool. A blue string is connected to the canteen and a chain holds the cork. This canteen was sometimes sold as a set of three which came in a box. The set contained a red, white and blue canteen. These covers are often stamped with information of a particular event. Because, the canteens were covered with felt or wool, many are now found faded or have deteriorated.

### Portrait Canteen

This generic canteen has a gold cover. In the center is a portrait of a Civil War General. The portrait is surrounded by the motto, "We Drank from the Same Canteen", and "1861-1865". This wording has faded. The use of pictures on canteens is not uncommon. A number of canteens have been observed with a portrait or battle scene. This includes a canteen manufactured in Gettysburg with the portrait of Jennie Wade. A chain holds a large cork.

### Portrait Canteen

This red canteen has a portrait of a Civil War General in the center. Unlike the previous canteen, this canteen was designed with a center depression for the portrait. This depression encircles the picture. Around the edge is the motto, "We Drank from the Same Canteen" and the dates "1861-1865". The ink has faded and is not very legible.

**The Croukle (?) Brigade**

This is an example of a canteen where the cover and stamping are quite faded. Much of the information is unreadable. However, the date of Sept. 23-24, 1891 and Des Moines, Iowa, can be read. The back stamping is clearer. The brown cover has crossed flags and the motto, "We Drank from the Same Canteen", and "1861-1865". The cork is present, but the chain is gone.

**Common Canteen**

This canteen has a light brown cover. The common design was sold at many events. It has the membership star with large G.A.R. letters. Around the edge is the motto. On the back, a veteran has drawn a Confederate flag and written his name, V.J. Green and ??? R. I. Below this, the veteran drew a musket.

**Monument Dedication**

This canteen was produced for the dedication of a monument in New Haven, Conn., June 17, 1887, by the Soldiers and Sailors Association. The center of the canteen has a view of the monument.

The back of the canteen has the standard membership star with G.A.R. letters and the motto, "We Drank from the Same Canteen", and the dates "1861-1865". The covering on this canteen is brown with a blue cord.

**Common Canteen**   **Reed City (Front)**   **Reed City (Back)**

The first common canteen would be sold at many events. The yellow covered canteen has a red cord. A chain connects the cork to the canteen. On the front is the G.A.R. monogram and surrounding this is the motto, "We Drank from the Same Canteen". A decorative circle completes the design.
Courtesy: G.A.R. Museum, Springfield, Ill.

The second canteen was made for the Soldiers & Sailors Association, N. W. Michigan. The center of the canteen has "Annual Reunion Reed City". On the back of the canteen is the motto, "We Drank from the Same Canteen", along with the intertwined G.A.R. letters. It is difficult to determine the original color of this canteen.

**117th New York Volunteers**

This simple canteen is stamped 35th Anniversary 117th N.Y.V. The reverse has a Corp badge stamped on it; the emblem of the 10th Corp. The front cover is light blue while the back has faded and deteriorated. The canteen has a blue cord but is missing the chain and cork. The 117th was organized in 1862, in Oneida County. The regiment was mustered in for three years. It participated in the defense of Washington, Peninsula Campaign, Fort Wagner, Cold Harbor and Petersburg. The lost in battle, 9 officers and 129 enlisted men. The Regiment mustered out June 8, 1865, in Raleigh, N. C.

### Abraham Lincoln Post No. 11            The Old Friend

**Lincoln**: This canteen is a souvenir that was made for the Abraham Lincoln Post No. 11. This Post was located in Charlestown, Mass. In the center of the canteen are crossed flags. The reverse has the membership star with G.A.R. in the middle. Encircling the star is the motto and dates. The cover is blue. It retains its cork and chain.

**The Old Friend**: This 3 inch canteen has a beautiful stamping of two wounded soldiers lying on the battlefield sharing a canteen of water. Around them are the clutters of war. The title is simply, "The Old Friends", and the date, "61 to 65". The covering is blue and nothing appears on the reverse.

### 25th Anniversary 1891
This double sided canteen is red on one side and dark blue on the other. It was made for the 25th Anniversary of the Order, 1891. The red silk has been stamped with a silver background. Around the center is, "Grand Army of the Republic-Organized April 6, 1866". The reverse is dark blue silk which has silver letters. It has the G.A.R. monogram surrounded by the motto and date.

### Blue & Gray Reunion
The miniature canteen on the right has a canvas cover. The cover has a lot of deterioration which makes the inscription hard to read. It is brown on one side and blue on the other. The front has, "Reunion of the Blue & Gray, Sept. 20, 21, 22, 23, Evansville, Indiana, 1887". On the back are intertwined G.A.R. letters and the motto, "We Drank from the Same Canteen".

34

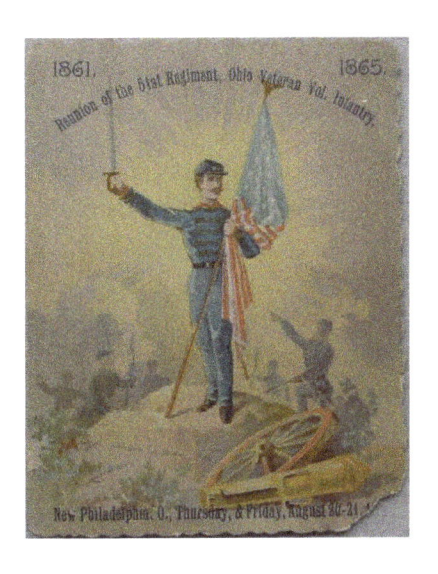

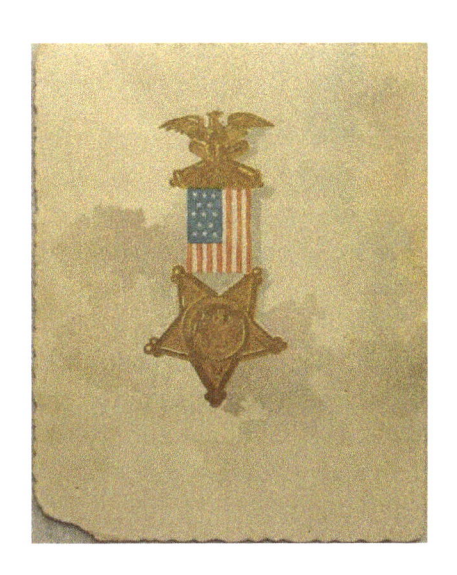

## 51st Ohio Veteran Volunteer Infantry

These two cards were probably once connected. They appear to be the front and back of a booklet for the 51st O.V.V.I. reunion which was held in New Philadelphia, 1891. The front has a soldier in blue holding a sword and flag. At the top is printed, "1861 &1865" and "Reunion of the 51st Regiment, Ohio Veteran Volunteer Infantry". At the bottom is, "New Philadelphia, O., Thursday & Friday, August 20-21, 1891". The other card has the membership badge of the G.A.R. The back of these cards has the following information. Cards Courtesy: Kathie Roussin

### Headquarters 51st Regiment, O.V.V.I.
New Philadelphia, O., August, 1891
General Order No. 1
The Committee having fixed the time and Place for the next reunion of this organization, You are hereby notified to report to these head Quarters on
August 20 and 21, 1891,
To greet your comrades of the late war. Comrades not attending in person, will be Required to report by letter to the secretary.
By command of
I. A. Correll          Samuel Slade
Secretary             President

### Officers

Samuel Slade, President
I. A. Correll, Secretary
C. C. Welty, Treasurer

Committee of Arrangements
C.C. Welty,          I. A. Correll,
George Dunn,       Reverdy Kirby,
O. P. Scott

### 51st O.V.V.I.
This double sided souvenir canteen was made for the reunion of the 51st O.V.V.I. The silk cover is blue and red. On the front is reunion information and the reverse has the G.A.R. monogram with the motto. The 51st O. V. V. I. was organized in late 1861 for three years of service. It was quite active, participating in the battles of Perryville, Stone's River, Chickamauga, Atlanta, Nashville and others. The regiment was mustered out in Texas, October, 1865.

## Metal Canteens or Flasks

The miniature canteen was a favorite souvenir for the Civil War veteran, but it was not the only type of canteen sold to them. A larger canteen was also produced as a souvenir. These canteens were generally 4 ½ inches across and were designed to hold a liquid. The type of liquid depended on the veteran's preference. Hence, these canteens are often referred to as "whiskey flask". The motto, "We Drank from the Same Canteen", had a real significance to many of the veterans as they attended Annual and National Encampments.

Like other souvenirs that were produced for the Grand Army, the canteen flask had generic designs that were sold repeatedly. Many designs had special information on particular Encampments. Some canteens were too large to be considered a whiskey flask and the veteran simply purchased them as a souvenir of that event. A few canteens were covered in cloth and leather. Regardless of the size or covering, the veteran carried and displayed his canteen with pride.

### Montezuma Rye Whiskey

This polished canteen is 4 ½ inches in width. A large 2 5/8 inch brass disk or medallion covers the front. The disk is quite elaborate with a rope border, scroll ribbon, wheat sheaves, bows and flowers. The disk says, "Celebrated Montezuma Rye Whiskey". The reverse of this canteen has a black leather cover. A small Grand Army membership badge has been cut out and glued to the center. This may have been added by the veteran. The canteen is believed to have been made by James Maguire, 470 & 472 N. 3rd St., Philadelphia, Pa. The trademark would have been stamped on the back but the cover hides it. The Montezuma trademark was used after 1875, and the James Maguire trademark from 1872-1900.

### Canfield's Phila

This is a smaller version of a metal canteen. It is 3 ½ inches across and has nickel plate. The center has a brass oval disk or medallion with "Canfield's Phila." printed on it. The medallion measures 1 ½ inches. A chain once held the cork to the canteen but is now missing. No makers name appears. This canteen was probably made for a bar or saloon and given out or sold to the veterans at one of the Philadelphia Encampments. This probably was a technique used to entice the veterans to frequent that establishment.

### Gettysburg

This small drum canteen has a screw top. There was probably a strap at one time but it is no longer present. The canteen has a nickel finish which is quite worn. On the face is stamped, "Gettysburg, July, 1863" and below this in large block letters is "G. A. R." It is not known if this was produced by the Post in Gettysburg for one of their encampments. It could have been sold as a souvenir at one of the many stores in town. Thousands of veterans, each year, visited Gettysburg.
Courtesy: Joan Radcliff

### Common Canteen

This common metal G.A.R. canteen measures 4 3/8 inches. The small medallion is 1 5/8 inch. It has the G.A.R. monogram of intertwined letters. The disk has the word "Patented" under the letters which appear in a straight line. A small loop at the base of the neck connects the chain and cork stopper. Stamped in the center on the reverse is the maker's name. This canteen was made by A. Ledig & Son, Phila., Pa. A small piece of blue chord is still attached. This canteen was made with several minor variations that can be found on the disk.

### Common Canteen

This canteen is very similar to the one above. One difference is the stamping which is found on the disk. On this canteen the word "Patented" is arched below the intertwined G.A.R. letters. Another difference is the length of the spout. This spout is shorter. The canteen is quite tarnished with age. The medallion is a chocolate brown color. The chain and cork are missing.

### Common Canteen

This Ledig & Son canteen is the largest G.A.R. metal canteen produced. At first glance, it looks like the other canteens, but, it measures 6 ¼ inches. It has an ornate copper disk in the center with the intertwined G.A.R. letters. Below the G.A.R. letters the word "Patented" appears in arched letters. The canteen still retains it chain and cork.

## Brass Canteen

This canteen has a brass finish. It was made by A. Ledig & Son, Philadelphia. The canteen is 4 3/8 inches. It has the standard 1 7/8 inch medallion in the center with the fancy monogram letters. On the reverse, a second medallion has been added. This disk has the coat of arms of the State of Pennsylvania. The seal has an eagle and rays with two horses with the state motto, "Virtue, Liberty, Independence". The chain is still attached, but the cork is missing. A frail yellow cord is attached. The canteen was made for either veterans of Pennsylvania at one of the Annual Encampments, or to commemorate a National Encampment held within that state. During its existence at least six National Encampments were held in Pennsylvania.

This canteen from A. Ledig & Son is almost identical to the previous one. The medallion on the back is double stamped with "Patented" on the left and "A. Ledig & Son" on the right. This appears just above the horses. This disk shows greater detail. While probably made for the same event as the one above, this shows some of the variations that the collector might encounter. The canteen has a red and gold cord.

39

## 26th Grand Annual Encampment

In 1892, the National Encampment of the Grand Army was held in Washington, D.C. A. Ledig & Son produced canteens for this event. One canteen was in a gilt color, while the others were nickel plate. Ledig changed the style of these canteens by enlarging the central medallion from 1 5/8 to 2 5/8 inches. The disk had a rope border. On one side appeared the portrait of three generals, Grant, Sherman, and Sheridan. Below the generals in large script are G.A.R. letters. Under this, are the Civil War dates, "1861 to1865". The date, "1892", refers to the encampment. A patent date of April 16, 1889, is present. The reverse has another large medallion with engraving of the National Capitol building. The disk says, "Souvenir-Twenty Sixth Grand Annual Encampment-Washington, D.C.-Sept. 20th to 23rd, 1892". It is interesting to note that it is referred to as the Grand Annual Encampment rather than the 26th National Encampment. The National Encampment badge for that year also portrayed the National Capitol building. The canteen still retains its blue cord, chain and cork. A small brown tassel has been attached to the cord.

This canteen for the 26th Grand Annual Encampment is identical to the one above with the exception of having a polished finish. The large medallion with the generals will be used again with other dates. The Capitol building will also be used with minor variations of the wording.

### 26th Grand Annual with Hat Cord

This example of the 1892, 26th Grand Annual, is shown with a Civil War hat cord.  This cord was probably added by a veteran.
Courtesy:  Joan Radcliff

### 26th Grand Annual Encampment with Corp Badge

This example of the 26th Grand Annual Encampment has the original leather strap.  Attached to the strap is a metal tag with a clover leaf Corp badge.  This was the emblem of the 2nd Corp.  The back of this canteen has a different medallion.  Instead of the three generals, it has a large disk with a keystone in the center.  Inside the keystone is the membership star with G.A.R. and the motto, "Fraternity, Charity, and Loyalty".  Surrounding this is the motto, "We Drank from the Same Canteen, 1861-1865".  This medallion will appear on canteens made for other encampments.  The keystone is one of the emblems of the state of Pennsylvania.  This canteen could have been made for Pennsylvania veterans.   Courtesy:  Joan Radcliff

**26th Grand Annual Encampment with Red, White, & Blue Cord**

Here is another example of the 1892 Grand Annual Encampment Canteen. The copper disk shows a lot of dings and is discolored in places. Overall, the canteen is in good shape. It still retains its original cork stopper and chain. What makes this canteen outstanding is the original cord which is still attached. The fancy cord is red and has a red, white and blue tassel which his been knotted. Do to the fragile nature of these cords, to find one, in this condition, is rare.
Courtesy: Roger and Fran Heiple

**Common Canteen in Original Box**

This is a common G.A.R. canteen. It is extremely rare to find the canteen in its original box. These boxes were usually discarded but this box has survived and shows its age. It may be one of a few that still exist. The canteen has the intertwined G.A.R. letters on a brass medallion with a blue cord.
Courtesy: Roger and Fran Heiple

## 27th National Encampment 1893

In 1893, the National Encampment was held in Indianapolis. A. Ledig made a souvenir canteen for this event. He must have had medallions left over from the previous year, because, he recycled the three generals disk. This canteen has the portrait of the three generals on the front. A close inspection of the date shows that the number 2 has been re-stamped. The 2 is now a 3, but traces of number 2 remain. The company did change the back. The new medallion has, "Twenty Seventh National Encampment-Indianapolis-1893". A large monument dedicated to the Soldiers and Sailors is in the center. This canteen retains it chain and cork.

## 36th National Encampment 1902

The 36th National Encampment was again held in Washington in 1902. A. Ledig & Son revived the emblem of the National Capitol. The canteen has, "Souvenir-36th National Encampment G. A. R.-Washington, D.C.-Oct. 8th to10th -1902". The reverse of this canteen has the keystone with "Fraternity, Charity, and Loyalty - 1866". 1866 is the date the G.A.R. was founded. The keystone is surrounded by, "We Drank from the Same Canteen-1861-1865". The canteen has its original chain and cork and retains its gold cord.

## 49th National Encampment 1915

Washington, D. C., was chosen to hold the National Encampment in 1915. The canteen for this event again depicted the National Capitol. Keeping with the style of the previous encampments, the medallion had, "Souvenir 49th National Encampment-G.A.R.-Washington, D.C.-Sept. 29th-30th, 1915". The reverse used the keystone design. This canteen has its chain but the cork is missing.

## Canteen with Pictures

This canteen is unusual. Instead of the metal disk in the center, pictures have been added. On one side is a picture of Gaines' Mills, Va. In the picture are the ruins of the mill. The other side has a picture of a fort overlooking a river. The fort has two large cannons and a soldier. It is possible that the veteran added these pictures. Possibly, he may have been stationed at these locations during the war. The answer will never be known.

44

**Post 2 Philadelphia**

This is a smaller canteen made for Post #2 in Philadelphia. This canteen measures 3 ½ inches. It retains its chain and cork along with the original red cord. No makers' name appears but it was most likely made by A. Ledig & Son. Nothing appears on the back.

**Sons of Veterans**

A. Ledig & Son made canteens for many groups including this canteen for the Grand Army Auxiliary, Sons of Union Veterans of the United States of America. The Sons of Veterans held their Annual and National Encampments in conjunction with the G.A.R. encampments. The canteen has intertwined S. V. letters on the medallion with rays emitting from the center. The word "Patented" appears upside down at the top. The canteen has seen better days and is quite dinged up on the back where the maker's name appears.

**Society of the Army of the Potomac**
Of all the canteens made for the various Civil War veterans' groups, the Society of the Army of the Potomac canteen is the most unusual. At first glance, it appears to be a simple tin canteen made for the 13th Annual Reunion, which was held in Detroit, 1882. The face has intertwined S. A. P. letters which are surrounded with "13th Annual Reunion" and "Detroit, 1882". Upon closer examination, this canteen is not a true canteen. It is a large banquet favor with the evening menu. The spout of this canteen comes off, and the canteen is hinged at the bottom. The sides open up to display the menu for the evening. The paper menu has red and green fringe and is printed on both sides. This canteen is extremely rare. Courtesy: Roger and Fran Heiple

The above picture is how the canteen appears when open. Note the hinge and spout cap on this banquet canteen. The menu is quite extensive. The selections range from green turtle soup to an entrée of wild pigeon. The reverse side of the menu has banquet greetings and a small poem.

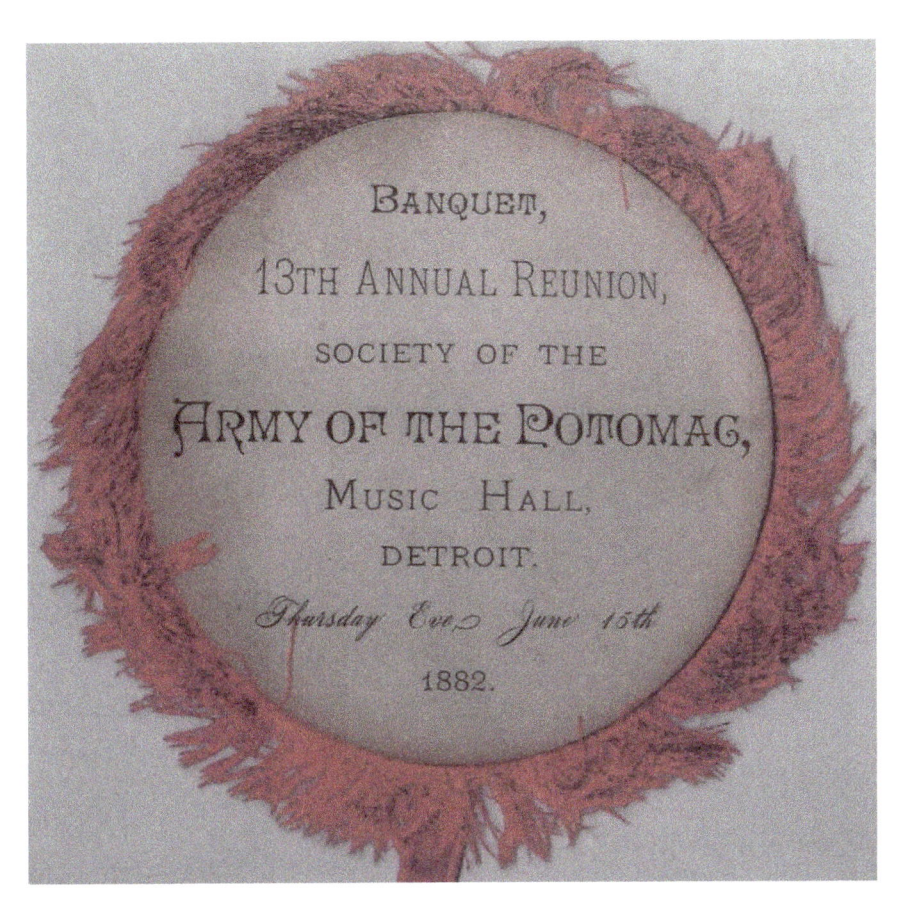

Upon opening the canteen, the veteran found the following cards which gave him selections for the evening meal along with greeting information.

**Banquet,**

**13th Annual Reunion,**

**Society of the**

*Army of the Potomac,*

**Music Hall,**

**DETROIT,**

*Thursday Eve, June 15th*

**1882**

"There are bonds of all sorts in this world of ours,

Fetters of friendship and ties of flowers,

And true lover's knots I wean.

The boy and the girl are bound by a kiss,

But there's never a bond old friends, like this,

We have drunk from the same canteen."

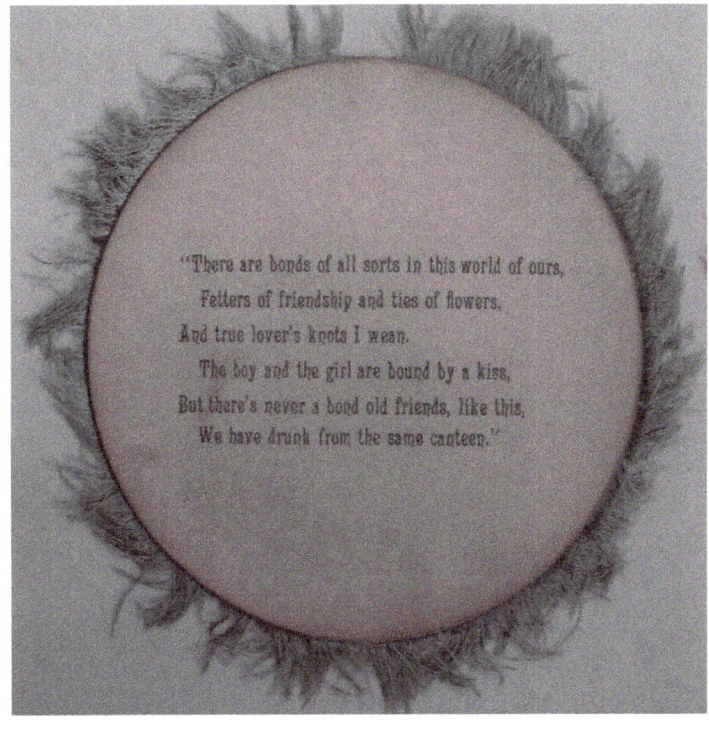

This poem ends with the motto, "We Drunk from the Same Canteen", used by the Grand Army. This is an example of the wide use of this saying by another veteran's organization.

**MENU**

Green Turtle Soup a l'Anglaise.

―――――

California Salmon, garnished a la Richelieu
Lake Superior White Fish, a la Canrobert.

―――――

Tomatoes      Cucumbers,

Ribs of Beef, a la Cardinal.
Saddle Southdown Mutton.
Roast Ham, Ornamented.
Roast Turkey, Cranberry Jelly
Spring Chicken, Roasted.
Boned Turkey, aux Truffes in Aspic Gelee.

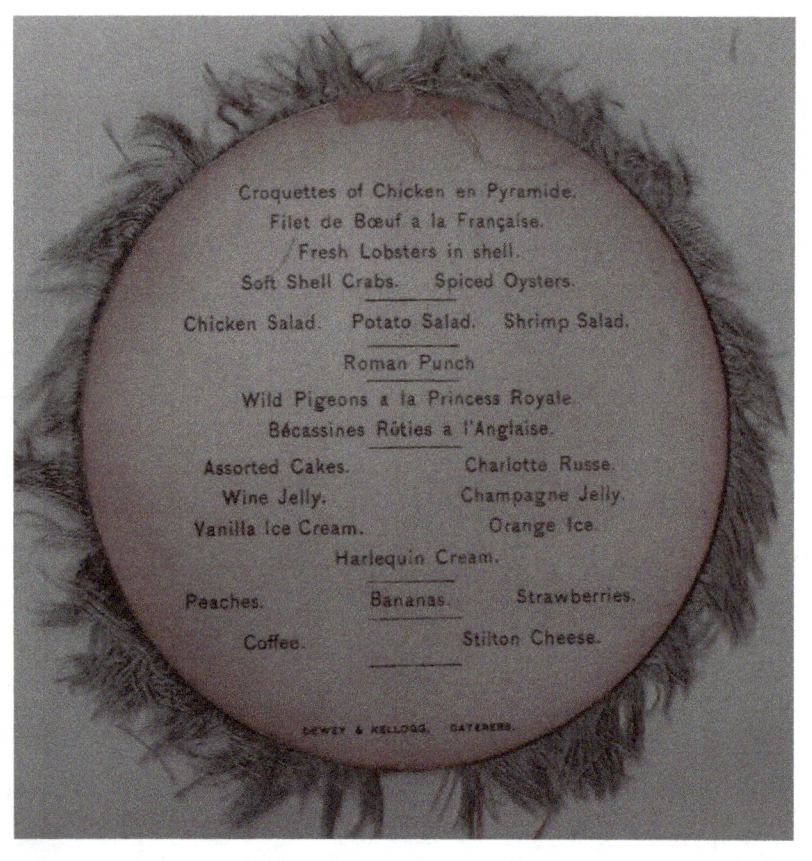

Croquettes of Chicken en Pyramids.
Filet de Boeuf a la Francaise.
Fresh Lobsters in shell.
Soft Shell Crabs.      Spiced Oysters.

―――――

Chicken Salad.  Potato Salad.  Shrimp Salad.

―――――

Roman Punch

―――――

Wild Pigeons a la Princess Royale
Becassines Roties a l'Anglaise.

―――――

Assorted Cakes.     Charlotte Russe.
Wine Jelly.         Champagne Jelly
Vanilla Ice Cream.  Orange Ice.
Harlequin Cream.

―――――

Peaches. Bananas. Strawberries.

―――――

Coffee    Stilton Cheese.

Dewey & Kellogg Caterers

The caterers, Dewey & Kellogg, gave the veteran an unbelievable amount of choices for this meal. By today's standards, a meal like this would cost hundreds of dollars. These veterans really knew how to party!

48

### Louisville 1895

In 1895, the 29th National Encampment was held in Louisville, Kentucky. 1,134 delegates attended. The canteen produced for this event differed greatly from the canteens previously made. These canteens measured 5 inches. Instead of the copper disk, they were enameled. The face of the canteen was white with a blue spout. The motto, "We drank from the Same Canteen", encircles a Federal eagle. It is holding olive branches and arrows in its claws. Below the eagle is "Louisville, 1861-1895". The back is white enamel and has no design. These canteens are often found with chips on the enamel. To find one in pristine condition is rare. This canteen has a red and white cord.

### Chicago 1900

The Chicago National Encampment of 1900 was a great success. More the 1,200 veterans and their families attended. There were parties, parades and banquets along with business meetings and other activities associated with G.A.R. Encampments. The canteen produced for the event was the same as the Louisville canteen five years before. It is an enameled canteen with an eagle in the center and the motto, "We Drank from the Same Canteen". On the bottom is printed, "Chicago, 1900", on a brownish gold field. The maker of this canteen must have had stock left over from the Louisville encampment. It appears he repainted the bottom of the canteen and added "Chicago, 1900". The interesting thing about these recycled canteens is the fact that the word "Louisville" has bled through some and can be seen under the word Chicago. This canteen has the original stopper and a red and white cord.

**Porcelain Canteen**

This canteen is the same size and shape as the Louisville and Chicago canteens. The canteen is white porcelain with blue trim. On the front is a large membership star which has been applied to the surface of the canteen. The star is made from stamped fabric. A red and white cord is attached.

**Blue Metal 1871**

This unusual canteen measures 5 ½ inches in width. It was probably painted by a veteran to be carried in parades or it may have been a souvenir from the war. Regardless, this canteen is crude when compared to others. It is hand-painted blue. The large G.A.R. block letters and date 1871 are white. The back has, "J. L., Co. F, 63". These are the initials of the veteran, with his company and regiment identified. Two of the strap holes are missing. A white canvas ribbon has been attached.

### Leather Canteen

This canteen measures 4 ½ inches. The surface of the canteen is covered with brown leather. The leather has been embossed. In the center is a large membership star. Around the star is the motto, "We Drank from the Same Canteen". This design appears on both sides of the canteen. The unfortunate thing about many of these canteens is the stamping is faded and only faint traces of the original stamping remain. This canteen has the original cord

### Leather Canteen with Violets

A light brown leather skin covers this canteen. It is possibly deer skin which has been stitched with a yellow thread. The front has been hand painted with blue violets. Around the edge in gold paint is the motto, We Drank from the Same Canteen". The canteen retains its original chain and stopper.

51

## Black Covered Canteen

This canteen is not the usual type of G.A.R. canteen. It is home made! Plain black material has been embroidered with a flower pattern. At the top appear the initials "M. C.". These are probably the owner's initials. The letters "R. G." and "67" are located at the bottom. These letters and number may represent a regiment. Its true meaning was known only to the veteran. The material has a blanket stitch around the rim. Pinned to this canteen is a G.A.R. membership badge with the bottom star missing. This appears be an original Civil War canteen. The cover was probably made by the wife or daughter of a veteran. Even though crude---it's the thought that counts.
Courtesy: Todd Rittenhouse

## Indian War Canteen

This is probably a surplus Indian War canteen which was recycled for a G.A.R. event. The canteen is regulation size (8 inches). It has a canvas cover which has been dyed light blue. On the cover, in large letters, has been stenciled G.A.R. A matching blue cord with tassels is attached. Possibly a hat cord was used for this purpose. Both the canvas and cord remain in near mint condition.

### Metal Grave Marker Canteen

To the right is a rusty metal grave marker in the shape of a canteen. There were many sizes and shapes of markers that were placed on the veteran's grave. Included in these was this metal canteen. This particular marker was made exclusively for the members of General John Segwick, Post 37, located in York, Pa. The dates 1861-1865 appear at the bottom. Grave markers are commonly seen at Civil War shows and at flea markets. These are not necessarily stolen from grave sites. Over the years, cemeteries simply removed and disposed of old rusted markers, many of which have been damaged like this one. Many markers have been rescued from cemetery flower dumps. Some G.A.R. post had a surplus of items including grave markers when the Post went out of existence. These were given away or sold and have survived in attics, sheds, and barns. And of course, their are the few who see a quick dollar and remove them from gravesites. This marker had been broken and the cemetery caretaker probably threw it away.
Courtesy: George Finlayson

### G.A.R. Marker

This grave marker is in the shape of a canteen. It has "G.A.R." and "1861-1865". The canteen is painted black and has gold letters and numbers. This canteen marker was rescued and is preserved in the Philadelphia Grand Army Museum along with many others.
Courtesy: G.A.R. Museum, Philadelphia

# Glass Whiskey Flask

At the turn of the century, a wave of patriotism swept the country. The United States declared war on Spain. Boys from every state rushed to join the army. This was called The Spanish American War. The Civil War had ended a little more than 30 years before. Now, the North and South were fighting side by side. This war did more to reunite the country than had been accomplished previously. The spirit of patriotism led many regalia companies to produce items of a patriotic nature. These items included glass plates, sugar bowls, ties, handkerchiefs, buckles, and much more. During this time, whiskey distilleries designed patriotic glass containers (flask) with flags and other American symbols. Below are some of the glass designs of the period.

## OurHero

This flask was made during or just after the Spanish American War (1898-1899). The war is sometimes referred to as the "Splendid Little War". The above flask has the picture of Admiral Dewey with a title of, "Our Hero". This souvenir whiskey flask was sold at many events across the country, including G.A.R. encampments. The back of the canteen is embossed with the letters "U.S.". There are several variations of these canteens. Courtesy: Joan Radcliff

## G.A.R Glass Whiskey Flask

This glass whiskey flask was made at the turn of the century. The canteen had a screw cap. Originally, a red, white, and blue cord was attached at the side. A printed paper was glued to the surface of the canteen. Then, a domed glass cover was added. On this canteen, a large G.A.R. membership badge is surrounded by a wreath and flags. No other information is given for the event. It is a generic design which was probably sold at both Annual and National Encampments

Both of these canteen flasks were made for the 33rd National Encampment which was held in Philadelphia, Pa., 1899. The 33rd National Encampment had more than 1,100 delegates. It is unknown how many flasks were made for this event. But, there must have been a large number. The above canteens still retain their caps and red, white and blue cords. These flasks were sold at several locations. Note the advertisement at the bottom of the membership star. The flask on the left has "T. J. Victory, Hotel Waverly, 15th and Filbert St.". The other one has "H. Byer, S. W. Cor., 2nd and Walnut Sts.". Courtesy: Joan Radcliff

### 1895 Louisville Flask
While these flasks were not shaped like a canteen, they show the process of inserting a picture between two pieces of glass. These were produced for the 1895, Louisville, 29th National Encampment. There were more than 1,100 delegates attending this event. On the bottom is printed, "I. W. Harper's, Nelson Co. Ky., Whiskey". Two versions of this bottle were made. On one bottle appears a white background and the other is gold.

55

# Porcelain Canteens (Parlor Ornaments)

Of all the canteens produced for Civil War veterans, the porcelain canteens (sometimes referred to as ceramic) are most often associated with a particular veteran. This is because he could adapt these canteens with his name and other information. The information was often in gilt and might include his Civil War company and/or regiment. He sometimes added his Grand Army Post name and number. These canteens were made in a variety of sizes and could be purchased through the mail or at the encampments. Manufacturers advertised and sent out price guides. At encampments plain white canteens were sold along with ones with decorative designs. These canteens have the membership badge in the center, which are sometimes painted. The badge appears very light on some and bold on others. The background offered a variety of designs which included plants, flowers, vines and battle scenes. Sometimes the back of the canteen was painted. These canteens are considered a work of art and are highly prized by collectors. In fact, the manufactures refer to them as "Parlor Art". But, do to the fragile nature of the porcelain canteen, they are often found with breakage on the spout and belt loops (especially the bottom loop). These "Parlor Art" canteens are greatly valued when found in pristine condition.

**Small Porcelain Canteen**

This canteen is solid white with a 2 ¾ inch membership badge in the center. The canteen measures 7 inches. The membership badge is very faint. This small canteen has flat sides. The three belt loops are intact with no breakage. The original stopper is missing.

### Canteen with Stars
This plain white porcelain canteen is quite uncommon. The canteen measures 6 ½ inches across the face. The canteen has a nice clear membership badge. Forty one stars surround the badge in two rows. The spout has two rings giving the impression that it would have had a screw top. These rings are decorative and the canteen had a cork. The bottom belt loop has been broken and this is not uncommon on a porcelain canteen.

### Large White Canteen
This canteen style was made by John R. Johnson of Cleveland, Ohio. The canteen was advertised as regulation size. It is a large white canteen which measures 7 inches across the front. The prominent membership badge is under a scalloped neck collar. This souvenir canteen was sold at encampments. The belt loops remain but the stopper is missing. The canteen has a rounded front but is flat on the back.

### Brown Canteen
This is a large chocolate brown canteen. These canteens can be found in a variety of colors. This canteen is missing two belt loops. A small ribbon is attached.
Courtesy: Roger Coulton

### Burgundy Canteen
This 8 ½ inch canteen is burgundy with a glossy finish. The spout, belt loops, and membership badge are in gilt. Below the badge, large U. S. letters have been added. This canteen was made with only two belt loops and they are quite large as is the spout's opening. A one inch leather belt is attached to this canteen. The moldy belt is very bridle from years of storage.

**Painted Badge Canteens**

Right: This canteen was made by John R. Johnson of Cleveland, Ohio. This common canteen was sold at many G.A.R. events. It has a membership badge 3 ½ inches long. The eagle and star are gilt and the flag is painted red, white and blue. The belt loops are also gilt and a red cord has been attached.

Below: This is another version of the Johnson canteen. This canteen has the addition of two crossed rifles with bayonets. The canteen has its original stopper. To the right is an advertisement for the Johnson canteen. He refers to his canteen as "White Porcelain Decorated Soldier's Canteen, A Beautiful Parlor Ornament". His canteens were made for G.A.R., Union Veteran Legion, as well as other veteran's organizations

This poem appears on Johnson's advertisement:

"There are bonds of all sorts in this world of ours,
Fetters of friendship and ties of flowers,
And true lover's knots I ween,
The boys and girls are bound by a kiss,
But, there's never a bond old friends, like this,
We have drank from the same canteen"

59

### "We Drank" Canteen

This large 9 inch canteen has a gilt circle that goes around the entire circumference. The eagle and star that appear on the membership badge is gilt while the flag has been painted. On the top is the motto, "We Have Drank from the Same Canteen". At the bottom, in large script letters is G.A.R. A vine scroll decorative pattern is on each side of the badge. Gilt appears on the belt loops and neck. A red, white and blue ribbon has been attached. The gilt is worn in several places on this canteen which is not unusual.

### Dogwood Canteen

This beautiful canteen is a work of art. The canteen has a painted membership badge in the center. In the background is a Civil War camp or battle scene with soldiers, tents, cannon and a flag. Encircling the scene is a broken wheel which has dogwood branches and flowers. At the bottom are the letters G.A.R. There is gold trim on the neck and loops but, the bottom loop is missing. The canteen has its original stopper and chain.
Courtesy: Dan Mitchell

### 203rd Penna V. I.
D. M. Fasig added his name to this canteen. His name appears at the top in large gilt letters. Below his name is the membership badge with a painted flag within a gilt circle. Around the badge is "Co. A" and under this is "203rd Penna. V. I." (Pennsylvania Volunteer Infantry), with some scroll work. The neck and belt loops have gilt, but the bottom loop has been broken.

The 203rd was recruited from the city of Philadelphia and surrounding counties in September, 1864. They were immediately sent south to participate in the seize operations around Richmond and Petersburg. The 203rd participated in the battle at Fair Oaks. They were then sent on the 2nd expedition to capture Fort Fisher. The regiment was present at the surrender of Johnson's army in North Carolina. They were mustered out June 22, 1865. The 203rd Regiment lost 4 officers and 70 enlisted men killed and wounded with an additional seventy two men from disease.

### The Round Heads
This beautiful canteen was designed for a veteran of Company B, 100th Pennsylvania Veteran Volunteers, known as the "Roundhead Regiment". It was probably manufactured by John R. Johnson of Cleveland, Ohio. The red canteen features a soldier on guard with rifle and overcoat. He is standing in front of the camp. Below the scene is "Co. B, 100th P.V.V." and "Roundheads". It is trimmed in gold and retains its original stopper and red cord. All belt loops are present. The Regiment was organized from counties in S. W. Pennsylvania. This area had been settled by the Roundhead and Scotch/Irish Covenanters who had followed Cromwell during the English Civil War. This Regiment was recruited from their descendants.

The 100th P.V.V. Regiment was organized in August, 1861, and sent to Washington. During the next four years the regiment participated in many battles and campaigns. Here are a few of the battle honors of this regiment. They fought at South Mountain, Antietam, Bull Run, Fredericksburg, , Wilderness, Spottsylvania, North Anna, Cold Harbor, Petersburg, Fort Stedman, and Appomattox. There were two Medal of Honor winners from Petersburg. The Regiment mustered out July 24th, 1865. The Regiment lost 409 men from all causes. Courtesy: Dan Mitchell
Source: History of Pennsylvania Volunteers 1861-65 by Samuel P. Bates

### James H. Stanford

This is a simple white canteen trimmed in gold. It has the membership badge in a circle with scroll work. Gold trim also appears on the belt loop bars. One loop has been broken. It is not uncommon to find porcelain canteens with chip and breaks. This veteran put his name, J. H. Stanford and his unit, the 19th Ohio Veteran Reserve around the membership badge. James Stanford was 19 years old when he enlisted as a private, August 11, 1862. He was part of the 19th Ohio Light Artillery. He mustered out July 27, 1865, at Camp Cleveland, Ohio.
Courtesy: Brad Pruden

### Wm. Monaghan

This canteen belonged to William Monaghan. It was made to commemorate his service in Company F, 104th Ohio Volunteer Infantry. This information is set in a large gold circle. A vine of leaf and flowers decorate the back of this canteen. Many veterans' canteens were decorated on both sides. A black ribbon is attached.
Courtesy: Joan Radcliff

### 104th Ohio Volunteer Infantry

This canteen has a very simple design. The eagle and star on the membership badge have a bluish color. The flag is red, white, and blue. The name of J. C. Price appears at the top in gold with a rosette on each side. At the bottom is 104th O. V. I. The 1 has worn off do to scaring. The bottom belt loop bar has been broken and no design appears on the back of this canteen.
Courtesy: Joan Radcliff

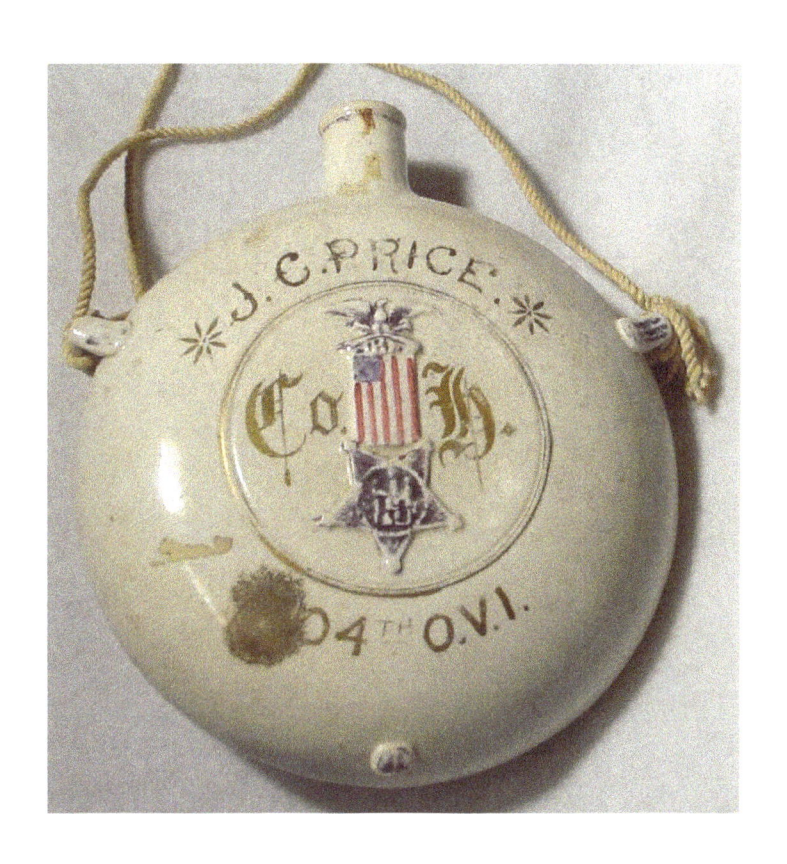

### 115th Ohio Volunteer Infantry

This is another Ohio canteen. The previous canteen and the 115th have similar designs, so they were probably painted by the same individual. This canteen commemorated the experiences of Lloyd Moore, Company L. of the 115th O. V. I. The canteen has survived very well with all belt loops intact. It still retains its original chain and stopper.
Courtesy: Joan Radcliff

63

### F. A. Irvin
This canteen belonged to F. A. Irvin. During the war, he was a member of Company L., 25th Iowa Infantry. This canteen has a painted G. A. R. badge surrounded by violets. It is trimmed in gilt. Flower designs seem to have been a favorite of veterans, because many of their canteens have been decorated with them.
Courtesy: Joan Radcliff

### 12th Michigan Veteran Volunteer Infantry
This canteen was made to celebrate the service of F. M. Rizer. He belonged to Co. A., 12th Michigan Veteran Volunteer Infantry. His name and company appear in script along with decorative designs. A golden eagle sits atop of a red, white, and blue flag. The membership star is also gold. This canteen has its original stopper and leather belt. The bottom belt loop has been broken and a piece of tape holds the belt.
Courtesy: Joan Radcliff

**Union Veterans Union**

Porcelain canteens were not exclusively made for the Grand Army. John R. Johnson of Cleveland probably made this canteen. Johnson extended his business to include other veterans' organizations, of which there were many. He designed and manufactured canteens with various insignias. This canteen has the membership badge of the Union Veterans Union. The U.V.U. badge has a red, yellow and blue ribbon. The pin bar has crossed swords and a star. Around this are the letters "U. V. U." and "1861-1865". The drop, on this badge has crossed rifles, cannon, and an anchor. These are surrounded with the words "Union Veterans Union". This canteen was made for John Cherry, Co. F., 1st. Regiment Hancock's Veterans.
Courtesy: The Horse Soldier

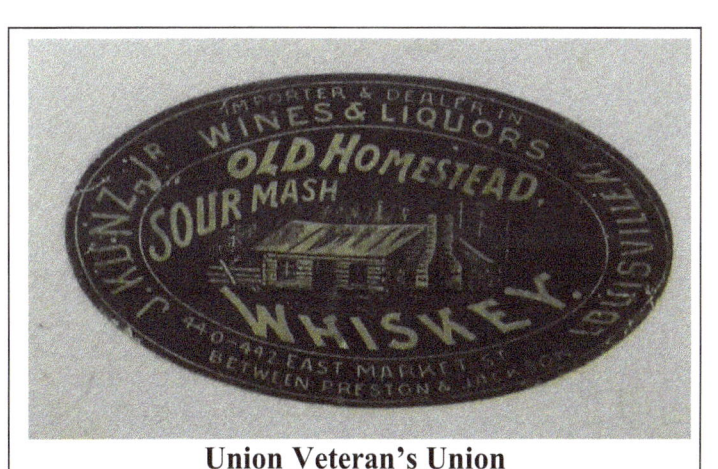

**Union Veteran's Union**
This plain white U.V.U. canteen was sold at the 29th GAR National Encampment held in Louisville, Ky., Sept.1895. Veterans who belonged to both organizations could purchase this canteen.

This canteen is rare because it still has its original stickers on the front and back. The shield has GAR and 29th National Encampment, Louisville, Ky., Sept. 1895. On the back is a black sticker with "Old Homestead Sour Mash Whiskey". There is no doubt what this canteen contained!
Courtesy: Dan Mitchell

## Union Veterans League

The U. V. L. was established in 1884, in Pittsburgh, Pa. The Union Veterans League was opened to all officers and enlisted men who had joined prior to July 1, 1863, for a term of three years (three year men). To belong, a veteran must have had an honorable discharge and served at least two of the three years. This canteen has the U. V. L. shield on its face. Around the edge of the shield is, "three year volunteers", and "1861*1865". In the center are the intertwined letters U.V. L. It is trimmed in gold with the name, "Wm. A. Clark, Butler, Pa.". The original red cord is still attached. Two U.V.L. badges are shown, one from Buffalo and the other from Washington. Courtesy: Leonard Shippy

### General Sherman

This souvenir canteen for General William T. Sherman is a commemorative piece which was made after his death. This canteen was sold at Annual and National Encampments as well as to the general public. The canteen is shaped like a drum with a gold trim and has the likeness of General Sherman. A small gold cord with tassels is attached. General Sherman died in New York City on February 14, 1891. His body was brought back to his home in St. Louis, Missouri, and is buried at Calvary Cemetery.
Courtesy: Roger and Fran Heiple

This canteen was made for the 50th Anniversary of the Battle of Gettysburg. The canteen is white and pictured is General Ulysses S. Grant on one side and General Robert E. Lee appears on the other. Even though Grant was not present at the Gettysburg battle, his picture is seen on the canteen. At that time, he was involved with the surrender of Vicksburg, a thousand miles away. Around his portrait in blue letters is, "The Blue and the Gray, In God Be Our Trust". With Lee's portrait, on the reverse is "Gettysburg, Pa., July, 1863, 1,2,3,4, July 1913". Thousands of veterans were in attendance for this famous battle reunion.
Courtesy: Joan Radcliff

### Small Ceramic Canteen
This small ceramic souvenir canteen measures about one inch. It does not appear to be a drop from any badge. The canteen is white and has G.A.R. letters on the face. A small red, white and blue ribbon is attached. It is thought to have been distributed or sold at one of the many Gettysburg Encampments.

### Jennie Wade
This red clay canteen celebrated the life of Jennie Wade. Jennie was the only civilian killed at Gettysburg. These canteens were supposed to have been made from clay found in Jennie's garden. It measures one inch. Jennie's portrait is found on the front of the canteen with the words, "correct photo, Jennie Wade". The reverse has, "killed at Gettysburg, the only lady" with the date "July 2, '63". It was a popular souvenir of the battle and several variations exist.

### Three Martyred Presidents

On this canteen is pictured the portraits of the presidents who have been assassinated; Lincoln, April 14th, 1865, Garfield, Sept. 19th 1881, and McKinley, Sept. 14th, 1901. These dates appear under each portrait. This canteen would be dated after 1901. The front of the canteen has the membership badge. This badge has been applied to the face and therefore, is not integral to the canteen. On the back of this smaller canteen is a portrait of each of the assassinated Presidents. Gold trim is found on the spout and the belt loop bars with a light blue cord attached. It was probably made for one of the National Encampments between 1902-1905.
Courtesy: Vann Martin

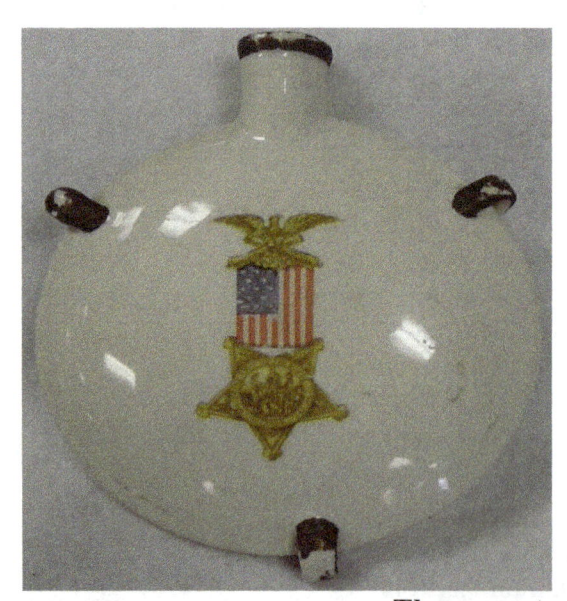

### Three martyred Presidents

With one exception, this canteen is identical to the one above. The spout and belt loop bars are trimmed in black. The bottom belt loop was not properly centered with the membership badge.
Courtesy: Leonard Shippy

### Department of Iowa

This smaller 3 ½ inch embossed stoneware canteen was designed with a flat base for standing upright in the parlor. One side of this canteen has, "26th Annual Encampment/ Department of Iowa/GAR/Davenport, Iowa/June 12, 13, 14, 1900". The reverse has "Compliments Aug. Wentz Post No. 1. / Davenport, Iowa". These words surround the letters G.A.R. and the Membership badge. The Wentz Post hosted this event and presented this canteen as a souvenir to the delegates. Originally, this canteen's letters were highlighted in blue, but, now only a trace of it remains. Part of the original cord is still attached, but, one loop has been broken. The maker's name, "Hinrichs Crockery Co. / Davenport, Iowa" appears in small blue letters on the bottom seam.

### Bud Vase/Whiskey Canteen

This unusual canteen has a flat bottom which allows it to stand upright on a table. This cream colored canteen is 6 inches high. The face has the membership badge of the G. A. R., 1861-1865. On the ribbon surrounding the badge is the motto, "We Drank from the Same Canteen". This is within a large gold circle. Embossed on the canteen are leaf patterns with a Dogwood flower. It may have been used for a flower vase but, more than likely it contained spirits. The true function of this canteen is unknown. Regardless, it is a beautiful example of a veteran's souvenir canteen.

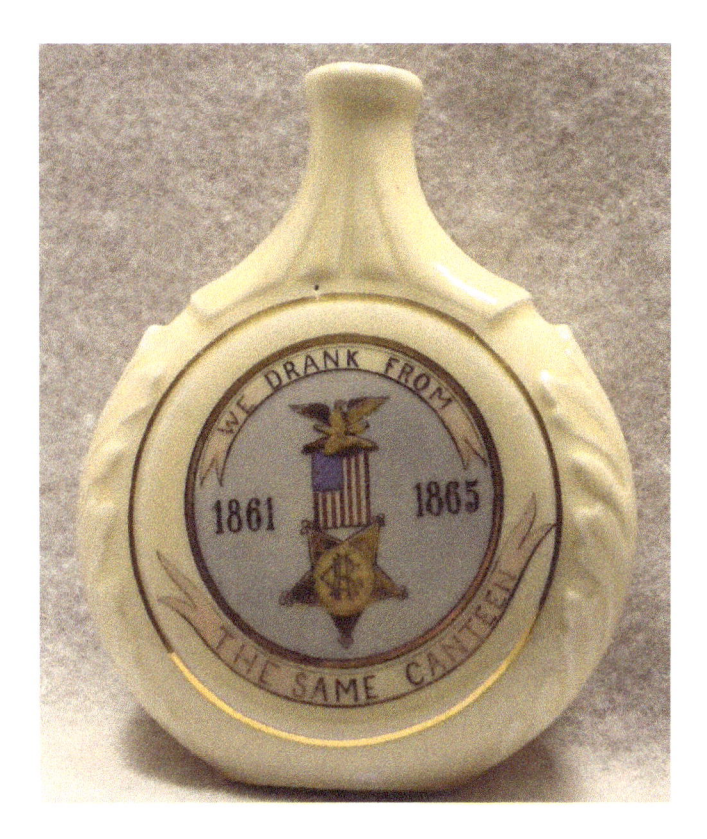

**Chicago Board of Trade Independent Light Artillery**

This canteen was made to commemorate Charles Holyland's service in the Civil War. He was a member of the Chicago Board of Trade Battery. John R. Johnson of Cleveland made this canteen which is trimmed in gold. The membership badge is on crossed cannon. The simplicity of this canteen design does not indicate the true history of this battery. The battery was mustered into service August 1, 1862, in Chicago and mustered out June 30, 1865. The Battery's original designation was Mounted Field Artillery. This was changed in March 1863, to The Flying Horse Artillery. It was attached to the Army of the Cumberland. Their battle honors include, the Battle of Stone's River, December 31, 1862 to January 2, 1863. During this battle, over 20,000 rounds were fired by the Union artillery. The Battle of Chickamauga, (September 19-20, 1863), and the Atlanta Campaign, (summer of 1864), were their next adventures. Later that year, they participated in the Battle of Nashville, December 15-16, 1864. The battery suffered light causalities. 10 enlisted men were killed in action or died from wounds. An additional 9 men died from disease.

The Chicago Board of Trade sponsored not only this battery but also, two regiments of infantry. The first Board of Trade Regiment was the 72nd Regiment, Illinois Volunteer Infantry, organized, August 23, 1862. The second regiment sponsored by the Board of Trade was the 88th Illinois Infantry Regiment. This regiment was called for duty September 4, 1862.

Chicago produced several independent batteries. Others include the Chicago Mercantile Battery of Light Artillery and Smith's Battery, Chicago Light Artillery.
Courtesy: Roger and Fran Heiple

### German Veteran's Canteen

Of all the canteens that appear in this study, this one was the most intriguing and frustrating. At first glance, it appears to be a plain white canteen with the G.A.R. membership badge across the front. It would have been sold at any Annual or National Encampment. When the canteen is turned over, it becomes very interesting. The back is a burgundy color with white letters. The wording on this canteen is written in old Gothic German script. This type of script was discontinued in Germany in the early 1900's. The name "Math Wein" (Mathias Wein) appears at the top with the word "Akron" (Ohio?). The Abbreviation, "Landw He'rr" also is found on the canteen. Consulting a number of German speaking residents, a literal translation is Military or Militia Men. The exact meaning is unclear as this abbreviation can be read several ways. Only the veteran knew its true meaning. Within the circle of words is a German Imperial Cross with the Gothic letters "R. D. B. U. A. The meaning of these letters is unknown.

71

Many badges other than the "Official Badge" were made for the 1892 National Encampment which was held in Washington, D.C. Examples would include Department badges, Post badges, Delegate badges and Souvenir badges.

<u>Top</u>: The badge at the top is from the Dept. of the Potomac. It is a bronze color which features a monument of Washington with Miss Liberty. The Capitol building is in the background.

<u>Left</u>: The badge on the left is a rare Palmer National Staff badge. This badge was worn in addition to the Official National Encampment badge.

## Washington, 1892

This canteen was sold during the 1892 National Encampment held in Washington, D.C. The canteen was made by John R. Johnson of Cleveland, O. It is trimmed in gold and has a red, white and blue flag. Behind the flag are crossed swords. Cavalry veterans would have been attracted to the canteens displaying crossed swords. This canteen has a faded brown ribbon but still retains it original stopper. As a generic piece, no name appears on this example. More than a thousand delegates attended this Encampment.

**Pittsburgh, 1894**

This colorful canteen was made as a souvenir for the 1894 National Encampment which was held in Pittsburg, Pa. A red circle surrounds the membership badge on the front of this canteen. The badge has a gilt eagle and star with a painted flag. Around this are the words, "Grand Army Encampment, Pittsburgh, Sept. 11$^{th}$, 94, in gilt. The outer part of this canteen is blue which surrounds the red and white circles. Each circle is outlined in gilt along with the spout and belt loops. This canteen still retains the fragments of the original red, white and blue ribbon. On the back, there is a gold circle which was probably intended for a name. It is unknown how many of these canteens were produced. But, do to the fragile nature of these "Parlor Art" canteens, few National Encampment canteens are known to have survived. There were more than 1,100 members of the Grand Army in attendance.

### Louisville, 1895

Souvenir Badge from Louisville

This canteen was manufactured for the 1895 Louisville, Kentucky, National Encampment. It is an elegant canteen in its simplicity. A baby blue color was used to accent this white canteen. The light blue color appears on the spout, belt loops and also on the membership eagle and star. To accent this color, the flag is painted red, white, and blue, with the tips of the star accented in gilt. The inscription is hand written. It has "GAR" at the top. Below this is "29th Encampment" and "Louisville, Ky". At the bottom of the canteen, is the membership star and date "1895". On the back of this canteen, in blue are the veteran's initials "C. H. W.". One other variation of this canteen has been observed in baby blue. The Commander in Chief of this encampment was Thomas G. Lawler of Illinois. The Grand Army had 45 Departments and a membership of over 350,000. 1,134 delegates* attended this Encampment.

* Membership and National Badges of the Grand Army of the Republic, 1866-1949, by Kenneth R. Johnson and Jeffery B. Floyd.

# HORSESHOES OF THE G.A.R.

The canteen was a popular emblem which had symbolic importance for the Civil War veteran. The emblem was used on ribbons and badges. Canteens were sold at events as miniatures, whiskey flasks, and as souvenirs. On Parlor Art Canteens veterans could have his name and other important information.

The canteen was a popular souvenir for the veterans of the Civil War, but, it was not the only one. Another popular souvenir of the late 1800's and early 1900's was the "Good Luck" horseshoe. The horseshoe design was used by many organizations. The Grand Army of the Republic, more than any other organization, was to distinguish themselves by the large number of horseshoe designs made for them.

Souvenir horseshoes of the Grand Army of the Republic fall into several categories.

### 1. Common Horseshoes:
The common horseshoes were generic in design. These
horseshoes were sold at many events and occasions.
They generally displayed the G. A. R. letters or some form
of the membership badge.

### 2. Special Events Horseshoes:
The special events horseshoes were made for a particular event
as an annual or national encampment or for other special occasions.
On the horseshoe would be displayed specific wording of the event.

### 3. I. D. (identified) Horseshoes:
These horseshoes were designed to be sold to the individual
veteran. The horseshoe might include the veteran's name, branch
of service, regiment, G. A. R. post number, or other pertinent information.

**HORSESHOE PENNYS:**

**LEFT:** This rolled penny was a souvenir of the 44th National Encampment held in Atlantic City, N. J., 1910. On the inside of the horseshoe are the words, "LUCKY CENT".

**RIGHT:** This penny was a souvenir for the 50th anniversary of the Battle of Gettysburg (1863-1913). Inside the horseshoe are a crossed American and Confederate flag. Below this are the words, "LUCKY CENT".

# COMMON HORSESHOES

**Good Luck**

This is a generic good luck horseshoe of the late 1800's or early 1900's. This was produced for any organization or sold as a souvenir piece to the public. While not specifically associated with the G. A. R., the basic design with an eagle on top will be the standard for many of the horseshoe souvenirs. This horseshoe measures 4 X 6 inches. It is made of iron and painted black with gold trim. The interior of the shoe has shaking hands in friendship with the wish of "Good Luck".

This G. A. R. horseshoe measures 4 X 7 inches. It is made of iron and has the eagle on top with spread wings. The eagle is facing its right. The center of the shoe has the G. A. R. letters on a circle with a star in the center which has a rosette. The eagle and interior are gold. The rest of the shoe is a grey color. It is not uncommon to have horseshoes painted and even glitter added. This shoe is painted with blue and red stars. The reverse shows a brass wire which allows the shoe to stand for display on a table.

### Sons of Veterans of the United States of America

By 1881, a number of Posts in the Grand Army had organized their sons into auxiliaries called the Sons of Veterans of the United States of America. Later, the name was changed to The Sons of Union Veterans of the Civil War. Many times, the auxiliaries held their Encampments in conjunction with the G.A.R. This horseshoe was a souvenir for several of these Encampments.

This souvenir follows the basic design of many G. A. R. horseshoes. The eagle is holding the membership badge of the Sons of Veterans. The badge ribbon is painted red, white and blue. The eagle and metal parts of the badge appear in a gold/brown color. The interior of the shoe is solid and painted black with large letters.

### Lynn Post Badge

The General Lander Post in Lynn, Mass., was a large Post and many things were made for their use, including this Post badge. The Badge on the left displays one of the industries of Lynn, the making of shoes. It is not uncommon for a G.A.R. badge to display local industries or landmarks. The pin bar is the sole. It has "Post 5 G.A.R. and Lynn, Mass". A red, white and blue ribbon connects a silver boot.

### General Lander Post # 5

This horseshoe was made for General Lander Post # 5. The Grand Army membership badge is draped across the front. The star rests on a printed ribbon with "Gen. Lander and Post #5". The eagle is missing from the top of the shoe and there is much rust which makes the inscription hard to read. The membership booklet, for this post, consisted of 30 pages and includes 1,124 names.

### Post Horseshoe

The horseshoe on the right measures more than 7 inches. It is made of polished iron which gives it a light grey color and shows no sign of paint. This eagle design is unusual because the wings are pointed downward and it is sitting on crossed rifles. The eagle faces its left. In the shoe, are G.A R. letters. The letters are above a wreath with a star in the center. Below the wreath is the word, "POST". A space was provided for a Post Number. These horseshoes have been observed with post numbers but none has been added to this particular one. A small hole has been drilled below the eagle so that this horseshoe could be attached to the wall or a display board.

This horseshoe is 6 ½ inches. The standard eagle is facing its right. The complete membership badge of the Grand Army is displayed inside this horseshoe. Below the badge are the letters G. A. R. The eagle and badge have been painted gold. Two small holes have been drilled in the shoe to allow its attachment to a wall or board. The reverse is marked, "DESIGN PAT APL'D FOR BY C. J. HOAG".

Hoag was a member of the firm, Whitehead and Hoag of Newark, N. J. The firm was established in 1892 and became famous. They produced medals, badges, ribbons and celluloid pins. The firm also manufactured many types of advertising items. By the turn of the century, it had become one of the largest companies in the world and employed several hundred workers.

78

The above is nearly identical to the previous horseshoe. The eagle is on top facing to its right. The complete membership badge is in the center of the shoe. Only the flag portion of the badge and the G. A. R. letters are painted. The reverse has, "DESIGN PT APL'D FOR". While not stated, this horseshoe was made by Whitehead and Hoag. The horseshoe is brass. Note the small hole on the back just above the membership badge. A wire was attached here to allow this shoe to stand on a table or cupboard.

### Artillery Horseshoe
This horseshoe was probably sold to a veteran who had served in the artillery branch of service. It has the eagle on top facing its right. The membership badge appears in the center but has been modified. The eagle has been removed and the cross cannons (artillery branch of service) have been enlarged. Notice the addition of the decorative bar at the bottom. This holds the membership badge in place. This horseshoe is made of brass and has not been painted.

This horseshoe measures 3 ½ X 2 ¼ inches and is much smaller and lighter than most shoes. The horseshoe is made of brass with the membership badge draped across the front and shows much detail. On the back, a ring has been attached, which allows the horseshoe to be hung. This ring could also indicate the horseshoe was part of a large badge at one time. The words, "I. M. Mayhem, Maker", appear on the back.

The horseshoe on the right measures 6 inches tall and 4 inches wide. The Grand Army of the Republic membership badge is draped across the front. The badge shows much detail especially in the eagle and flag. Arching below the membership star are the letters G. A. R. This horseshoe has not been painted and the makers name does not appear.

80

### Large Star
The standard eagle on this horseshoe is facing right. It has a simple design. An unusual feature of this shoe is the large membership star in the center. The area above the star is painted white and blue with red stripes. This represents the ribbon of the badge. Below the star is a saw-tooth bar with G. A. R. letters. A light gold glitter was used to highlight this design.

### The Union Forever
The horseshoe on the right has a brass color but is made from a softer material. It has G. A. R. letters at the top cradled in a wreath and the membership star is at the bottom. Cast around the edge are the words, "THE UNION FOREVER". The letter "T" is missing. On the shoe is inscribed, "YOURS IN F. C. & L.", (Fraternity, Charity, & Loyalty). A soldier stands guard near the flag. Sometimes these flags are painted, but this one is left unpainted.

81

### The Union Forever
The horseshoe on the right is quite unusual. Being made of pot metal, it is very soft. It is probably a recasting of an iron or brass horseshoe. The workmanship is very crude. This horseshoe has the G. A. R. letters at the top cradled in a wreath. The membership star is at the bottom. Cast around the edge are the words, "THE UNION FOREVER". The "T" on this shoe is also missing. Inscribed on the shoe is, "YOURS IN F. C. & L.", (Fraternity, Charity, & Loyalty). In the center, a soldier is guarding the painted flag. Three stripes appear on the flag. They are painted red, white, and blue. This horseshoe was originally painted black with yellow trim.

### Good Luck (Red)
The horseshoe on the left is made of iron. It is quite large measuring 5 ½ X 6 ¼ inches. On its face are the words, "Good Luck". The membership badge is draped down the center along with two tree trunks. At the bottom are the letters, "G.A.R.". At one time the horseshoe was painted red. Some traces of this paint remain. This shoe design was also used on larger parlor art horseshoes. Those shoes had tree trunks which formed an easel. On the easel was a faithful hunting dog keeping watch. This horseshoe was probably a modification of the larger shoe design.

### Friendship
This large, colorful, horseshoe on the right measurers 5 ½ X 6 inches. It is made of iron and is painted blue. In the center are G.A.R. letters. These letters are gold and the badge is red and white with a gold eagle. Finishing this design are shaking hands. A small flag is painted on the ribbon. Originally a large eagle sat on top. The missing eagle was the largest produced on any G.A.R. horseshoe. The shoe was probably dropped and the eagle was broken and lost.

### 1861-1865 Horseshoe
The horseshoe on the left has a design which is rare. It is a plain shoe, painted black with the dates "1861" and "1865". At the top is "F. C. L." (fraternity, charity, loyalty). Under this are the letters G. A. R. The membership badge is entirely within the shoe. The flag portion of the badge is unpainted while the eagle and star are gold.

### 20th Pennsylvania Cavalry
Here is a simple horseshoe design. On the face is "20th Regiment Pennsylvania Volunteer Cavalry". The shoe has no other information. This shoe is similar to the larger parlor art display horseshoes, but, is missing the veterans name and other information. It is possible that this shoe was made specifically for a reunion of the 20th cavalry.
Courtesy: G.A.R. Museum Philadelphia

83

## Good Luck with Dog

This is one of the largest and most ornate horseshoes made for the Grand Army. It measures 9 X 7 inches. The horseshoe is resting on an easel in the shape of tree logs. Sitting on the log is a gaunt-looking dog keeping guard. When first made, this horseshoe would have been taller. Originally the tree logs crossed at the top which gave it an additional inch or two. This portion has been broken off. The horseshoe has been painted gold, but, has been observed in a variety of colors. The membership badge is draped across the front. Below this are the letters "G. A. R." Both the badge and letters are not very detailed. The face of the shoe has the wish of "GOOD LUCK". This horseshoe was designed to stand on a table. The third leg is no longer attached.

(The Type 3 membership badge 1869 to 1876)

## **Horseshoe with Large Eagle**

Here is a very large and heavy horseshoe which was made for the Grand Army of the Republic. It measures 6 ½ wide and 8 ½ tall. It is made of iron with the largest eagle of any G. A. R. horseshoe. The eagle faces its left. The interior of the shoe has large G. A. R. letters which have been painted red, white, and blue. These letters surround the early Type 3 membership badge. This badge was made between 1869 and 1876. Note that the eagle's wings are pointed upward. After 1876, the membership eagle's wings were pointed to the side. The eagle and membership star are painted gold with a crudely painted flag. Below the star are two hands shaking in friendship. These have also been painted. The reverse has a hole which once held a large wire pin. This allowed this horseshoe to stand for display on a table. No maker's name is found.

85

### Grand Army R. with Broken Wing

The horseshoe on the left has the standard pattern of most G.A.R. horseshoes. It has the eagle on top and the shoe below. What makes this shoe different from most is, the addition of the words, "GRAND ARMY R.". The top of the letters are an intricate part of the casting. These letters were easily broken and this shoe is found many times with missing letters. The complete membership badge is found inside the horseshoe. In order to stabilize the badge, a bar was added to the bottom for support. The horseshoe is painted silver and the letters and eagles have a bronze color. The flag is red, white, and blue. The top eagle has a broken wing. This probably occurred from being dropped.

### G.A.R. Horseshoe with Bar

This horseshoe is painted black. It is a standard design with a large eagle on the top. The full membership badge is in the center of the shoe. Across the flag portion is a bar with the letters G.A.R. There is a hole under the large eagle for attachment to a wall. Two larger holes appear on the bar.

# SPECIAL EVENTS HORSESHOES

### 22nd National Encampment 1888

The horseshoe on the right was made for the 22nd National Encampment which was held in Columbus, Ohio, 1888. The eagle is on top and the complete Grand Army membership badge is in the center. Below the badge are the letters G.A.R. These letters have been painted red. On the horseshoe is the date, "1888", which has also been painted red. This is the only horseshoe, of this design, that has a date on front. A light red color appears on the eagle's wings. The horseshoe is made of brass.

### 22nd National Encampment 1888

This is another souvenir horseshoe that was sold at the 22nd National Encampment held Sept. 11, 1888, in Columbus, Ohio. 585 delegates attended this Encampment. The horseshoe was made to commemorate the Ohio Centennial, (1788-1888). The interior of the shoe has large G.A.R. letters. Under the letters are the words, "Columbus, O.". The horseshoe is made of brass and measures 6 X 6 1/4 inches. This shoe does not have a maker's name.

87

### Lincoln Horseshoe
The profile of Abraham Lincoln appears in the center of this horseshoe. "With Malice Toward None" is inscribed around his profile. A loop is at the top for hanging. The front has a bronze finish. This horseshoe is often overlooked as a Grand Army souvenir. But, in faint letters on the back is inscribed, "Commemoration of the 22nd National Encampment of the Grand Army of the Republic and of the Ohio Centennial, Sept. 1888, Columbus, Ohio".

### Lookout Mountain
This souvenir horseshoe was made for the 47th National Encampment held at Chattanooga, Tennessee, 1913. This horseshoe commemorates the great Civil War Battle of Lookout Mountain were the encampment was held. On the horseshoe is an eagle sitting on top of the complete membership badge with G.A.R. letters. On the face of the horseshoe is printed "Lookout Mt." The pin is still attached to the back and this allows the shoe to stand on a table.

### 23rd National Encampment 1889

This horseshoe was designed for the 23rd National Encampment. The Encampment was held in Milwaukee, Wisconsin, 1889. This date appears on the front. The entire horseshoe is painted gold. Perched on top, is an eagle facing its right. The inscription of the event and date are placed around the shoe. In the center of the shoe are the G.A.R. letters. These letters surround a star with a rosette. The tip of the eagle's wing is broken. There is also a break at the bottom. The letter G can still be seen. This was probably the first letter for Grand Army. The National Encampment held in Milwaukee had 641 delegates.

### Annual Encampment 1893

This simple horseshoe is 6 inches tall and made from iron. It was produced for the 27th Annual Encampment in Indianapolis, Indiana, 1893. On the reverse is inscribed the maker's name and address, "D HAIN--2541 Nth 7th". No city name is given.

## I. D. (identified) HORSESHOES (Parlor Displays)

Many veterans had a special "good luck" horseshoe personalized especially for them. Like the porcelain canteens, a veteran could have placed on the horseshoe his name, regiment, company, G.A.R. post number or other information. These horseshoes were designed to stand for display in the parlor. They measured approximately 10 to 12 inches tall and more than 6 inches across. Officer's horseshoes were designed differently. They were slightly larger and heavier than the enlisted man's. These horseshoes are highly desirable because they are associated with an individual soldier. The shoes were probably made by a company in Philadelphia. On the back is the name and address, "D. Hain, 2541 N. 7th". Often these shoes are associated with veterans from Pennsylvania.

### Captain Robert Gillespie

Captain Robert Gillespie was a member of the 26th Regular Pennsylvania Volunteers. This appears on the information bar at the bottom of the shoe. His name and rank circles the shoe. An eagle is on top of this horseshoe. He is facing his left. On the enlisted man's shoe, the eagle faces right. Appearing below the eagle is an officer's hat and sword and his Company letter. In the center is a G.A.R. membership star, below this is Post 51 with a canteen. Post 51 was the Capt. Schuyler Post and was located in Philadelphia. The legs of this display are in the shape of cannon barrels. The 26th Pennsylvania Volunteers were one of regiments that faced the Baltimore mobs in 1861. The regiment being unarmed was forced to retreat after one man was killed and several wounded. It was also known as the "Washington Brigade" because of its early defense of the Capital. The 26th participated in most of the major battles in Virginia, from the Peninsula to the Wilderness. It was mustered out June 18, 1864. Loses to the regiment were 8 Officers and 214 enlisted men.
<u>Source</u>: Website 26th Regiment Pennsylvania Volunteers

## 2nd Regiment U. S. Colored Troops (U.S.C.T.)

This rare 2nd Regiment U. S. Colored Troops parlor display was made for John W. Butler. The horseshoe is designed quite differently from an officer's horseshoe. The eagle on top is facing its right while the eagle on an officer's horseshoe is facing left. The enlisted man's horseshoe appears much thinner and the wording is reversed. Inside the shoe is a small membership star. Crossed rifles are below this with "Post 80" and the traditional canteen. A search for John Butler revealed numerous troops with that name. It is believed that Post 80 refers to the Robert Bryan Post. This Post was located in Philadelphia. The 2nd Regiment was formed in1863, Arlington, Virginia, at Camp Casey. The men were recruited from Washington, Virginia, and Maryland. These colored regiments were commanded by white officers. After the regiment was mustered, it was sent to the Department of the Gulf, December, 1863. This regiment garrisoned New Orleans. Later, they were attached to the District of Key West and then attacked the Confederate fortifications at Tampa. This regiment participated in several raids along the Florida coast from Fort Meyer to Bayport. The regimental loses were 3 officers and 24 enlisted men with another 11 officers and 135 enlisted men dying from diseases. Source: Website-2nd United States Colored Troops

## 39th Massachusetts Volunteer Infantry

William Nelson had this horseshoe made to commemorate his service with Company F, 39th Massachusetts Infantry. This horseshoe has his name on the information bar with his regiment across the shoe. As with most enlisted men's shoes, the eagle faces its right. Below this is the G.A.R. membership eagle and star with crossed rifles indicating infantry. Nelson belonged to the Department of Massachusetts, G.A.R. Post #3. This is the W. F. Barlett Post and was located in Taunton, Mass. While most horseshoes like this one are associated with Pennsylvania veterans, this particular one was produced for a veteran from Massachusetts. The reverse has the maker's name, D. Hain. This horseshoe has a gilt finish. The 39th Regiment was organized in August-September, 1862. The regiment was deployed to defend Washington, where it guarded river crossings along the Potomac. Later, it was sent to Harper's Ferry. In 1864, the regiment participated in many battles. These included the Wilderness, Spotsylvania, North Anna, and Petersburg. The regiment was present at Lee's surrender April, 1865. After the war, the regiment marched in the Grand Review. It was mustered out June 1, 1865. The regiment suffered 5 officers and 91 enlisted men killed or mortally wounded and 183 men died of disease.

Source: Website of the 39th Mass. Volunteer Infantry

## 112th Regiment Pennsylvania Volunteers 2nd Heavy Artillery

This horseshoe was made for William MacLardy who served in the 112th Regiment Pennsylvania Volunteers 2nd Heavy Artillery. The horseshoe has the eagle facing its right with the membership eagle and star. Below the star are crossed cannon, indicating an artillery unit. On the canteen is Post 7. This Post 7 was named after Captain William S. Newhall and was located in Philadelphia. The 112th was organized in Philadelphia. In February, 1862, Company C was sent to Washington and assigned to defend positions north of the city. These heavies remain in Washington until the spring of 1864. In May, 1864, the regiment was transported to Port Royal, there it joined the army of the Potomac at Cold Harbor. After this, they participated in seize operations at Petersburg and Richmond. The 112th was mustered out, January 29, 1866. Loses to the regiment amounted to 5 officers and 221 enlisted men killed or mortally wounded with 5 officers and 385 men from disease for a total of 616 men.

Source: Website, 2nd Heavy Artillery, 112th Regiment Pennsylvania Volunteers

## 8th Regiment Pennsylvania Volunteer Cavalry

This horseshoe was made for John H. Hagarty of the 8th Pennsylvania Volunteer Cavalry. The horseshoe bares his name and regiment. In the center of the shoe are crossed swords indicating cavalry. John Hagarty belonged to G.A.R. Post 56. This was the General Phil Kearney Post and was located in Frankfort, Penn. Note on the name bar, the A is missing. The letters and numbers were put on individually. Traces of gold paint remain on the shoe. The service record of John Hagarty indicates that he joined September 17, 1861, for a three year enlistment. He was assigned to Company E. His files show that he deserted, but later returned. After his return, he was re-assigned to a new company. This is why Company K appears on the horseshoe. He remained with this unit until the end of his enlistment and was honorably discharged on September 19, 1864. This honorable discharge allowed him to join the G.A.R. The 8th was organized September and October, 1861, in Philadelphia. The unit was sent to defend Washington. The 8th was very active throughout the war and were constantly on patrol duty. The unit was at Yorktown, Antietam, Fair Oaks, Chancellorsville, Gettysburg, Sheridan's Raid to the James River, Cold Harbor, Trevillian Raid and Five Forks. They were also present at Lee's surrender. The 8th Pennsylvania Cavalry was mustered out July 24, 1865. Loses were 5 officers and 55 enlisted men killed or mortally wounded and 2 officers and 126 men from disease.
Source: Website 8th Pennsylvania Volunteer Cavalry.

**The Naval Post**

Items associated with Navy veterans of the G.A.R. are quite rare. This horseshoe was made to commemorate the service of Laurence Naulty. The horseshoe indicates he was a sailor aboard the United States Steamships, "State of Georgia" and "Sciota". At the top of the shoe is "Post 400". This post was located in Philadelphia and was known as the "The Naval Post" because the members served in the navy during the war. There is evidence that the horseshoe may have had a center portion, but, it has been lost.

**State of Georgia**: The State of Georgia was a side wheel steamer. It was built in Philadelphia, 1851, for commercial trade. In 1861, the Navy Department purchased the vessel and refitted it for active service. The ship was assigned blockade duty along the coast of Virginia and North Carolina. It participated in this duty throughout the war. The ship was involved in the bombardment and capture of Fort Macon. After the war, the State of Georgia was decommissioned in New York City, September, 1865, and sold at public auction. The ship resumed its commercial trade under the new name Andrew Johnson. On October 5, 1866, the ship sank off the coast of North Carolina during a hurricane. It was a total loss.
Source: Wikipedia, "U.S.S. State of Georgia, 1851"

**Sciota**: The Sciota began its life as one of the "90 day wonders" built by the navy at the beginning of the war. It was commissioned at Philadelphia, December 15, 1861. The ship was assigned to the Gulf Blockade Squadron and arrived January, 1862. The Margaret, with its load of cotton, was the first ship captured by the Sciota. After this, it was assigned to Admiral David Farraguts's command. While under his command, the Sciota was involved in the capture of New Orleans. Later, the ship collided with the Antona on the Mississippi River and sank. It was raised and sent to New Orleans for refitting. In 1865, the ship was ordered to Mobile Bay to clear mines where it struck a mine and sank. The boat was again raised and sent to New York and sold at public auction.
Source: Wikipedia, "U. S. Sciota"

# Appendix

## Canteen & Horseshoe Manufacturers

The following is a list of dealers/manufactures that have been found on the Grand Army of the Republic badges, canteens and horseshoe described in this book. The companies are listed in alphabetical order. The names and information are listed as they appear on the badge, canteen and horseshoe.

### Badges
1. Heeren Brothers & Co., Pittsburg, Pa.
2. The Whitehead & Hoag Co., Newark, N. J.
3. Schwaab S. & S. Co., Milwaukee
4. S. D. Childs & Co., Engravers, Chicago
5. Wm. R. Brown, 45 Eddy St. Providence, R. I.

### Crockery
Hinrich Crockery Co., Davenport, Iowa

### Porcelain
No name appears on the Porcelain canteen, but it is known to have been made by John R. Johnson of Cleveland, Ohio.

### Metal Canteens
A. Ledig & Son, Philadelphia, Pa.

### Metal Horseshoes
1. D. Hain, 2541 N. 7$^{th}$
2. Design Pat. Apl'd for by C. J. Hoag
3. I. M. Mayhem, Maker

# Bibliography

A Collectors Identification and Price Guide for the Grand Army of the Republic Memorabilia, Dennis M. Gregg, Full House Publications, 2005

The Civil War, A New Six-part series on our Nation's bloodiest Drama, Life Magazine, June 1961

Membership and National Encampment Badges of the Grand Army of the Republic, 1866-1949, Kenneth R. Johnson and Jeffrey B. Floyd, OMSA Monograph, 1997

Plates, Belts and Swords of the Grand Army of the Republic and Sons of Union Veterans of the Civil War, Douglas Roussin, Graybird Publishers, 2008

## Websites:

James Maguire Co. Philadelphia, Pa. 1872-1915
The Society of the Army of the Potomac
203rd Pennsylvania Volunteers
100th Pennsylvania Volunteers, The Roundhead Regiment
19th Ohio Volunteer Light Artillery
Unions Veteran's Union
General Wm T. Sherman
Chicago Board of Trade Independent Light Artillery
26h Regiment Pennsylvania Volunteers
2nd Regiment United States Colored Troops
39 Massachusetts Volunteer Infantry
112th Regiment Pennsylvania Volunteers 2nd Heavy Artillery
8th Regiment Pennsylvania Volunteer Cavalry
United States Steamer State of Georgia
United States Steamer Sciota

# ABOUT THE AUTHOR

　　　　Douglas Wayne Roussin is a native of DeSoto, Missouri, and was an Elementary School Teacher for 34 years.

　　　　Doug has collected Civil War and Grand Army of the Republic memorabilia for nearly 60 years. He began his collecting career at the age of 9 when he found his first Native American arrowhead on his father's farm. He became interested in the Civil War after finding trenches on the hills around his home in DeSoto. During the Centennial, he began collecting Civil War rifles, swords and belt plates.

　　　　After graduating from Southeast Missouri College in 1970, he discovered metal detecting and began digging at a local battlefield. Years later, he was part of a committee which erected a monument to the brave men who fought there.

　　　　Years of collecting Civil War relics led to the discovery of the G. A. R. and other veteran's organizations. He expanded his collecting to include buckles and swords of the Grand Army. This in turn led to his first book "Plates, Belts, and Swords of the Grand Army of the Republic and Sons of Union Veterans of the Civil War". Canteens and Horseshoes is his second title.

　　　　Doug currently belongs to the "Civil War Veterans Historical Association", a national collectors club. He also is the Commander of "General Thomas C. Fletcher, Camp 47, Sons of Union Veterans of the Civil War" in DeSoto.

　　　　Doug's wife, Kathie, has always shown an interest in his hobby and is quite knowledgeable in her own right. She has accompanied him to antique and relic shows around the country. Now, that both are retired, they enjoy traveling and especially cruises. And of course they still spend time with Civil War activities and searching antique and relic shows for that rare piece of history.